Fashion Means
Your Fur Hat
Is Dead

Fashion Means
Your Fur Hat Is Dead

*A Guide to Good Manners
and Social Survival in Alaska*

Mike Doogan
Illustrated by Dee Boyles

Epicenter Press
Fairbanks / Seattle

Epicenter Press Inc. is a regional press founded in Alaska whose interests include but are not limited to the arts, history, environment, and diverse cultures and lifestyles of Alaska and the Pacific Northwest.

Publisher: Kent Sturgis
Acquisitions Editor: Lael Morgan
Cover design: Leslie Newman
Text design: Sue Mattson
Cover & Text illustrations: Dee Boyles
Proofreader: Lois Kelley
Printer: Transcontinental Printing

PRINTED IN CANADA
10 9

To order single copies of FASHION MEANS YOUR FUR HAT IS DEAD, mail $14.95 plus $6 for Priority Mail shipping (WA residents add $1.85 state sales tax) to: Epicenter Press, PO Box 82368, Kenmore, WA 98028, phone our toll-free order line at 1-800-950-6663, or order online at www.EpicenterPress.com. Visit our online Alaska art gallery featuring Jon Van Zyle, member of the Iditarod Hall of Fame, at www.JonVanZyle.com.

This book is for my parents,

Jim and Jerry Doogan,

who are the reason

I am an Alaskan.

Contents

Introduction. **11**

Chapter 1: Coming Into the Country. **14**
Or, Are You Sure This Is a Good Idea?

Your first visit: How to survive in Southeast Alaska, which smells like wet wool, and in Fairbanks, where sophistication means your socks match. Anchorage? *Never* say anything nice about it.

Chapter 2: Home Is Where the Heart Is. **24**
Or, Creative Use of Dead Animals and Broken Appliances

Rules for decorating your home: An Alaska home contains more dead animals than live people. You must have a car on concrete blocks or a used appliance in the front yard.

Chapter 3: Finding a Job. **36**
Or, How to Compile an Alaska Resume

Consider doing nothing, which Alaskans do so well. Take a government job only as a last resort, and if you do, start looking right away for a job with more status.

Chapter 4: An Alaskan Is as an Alaskan Does . . **44**
Or, How to Become Rude, Crude, and Well-Equipped

Complain about the government, the weather, new arrivals, and tourists. Collect dogs and guns. Understand the difference between "gear" and "stuff."

Chapter 5: Surviving the Outdoors. 54
Or, Are Tourists Worse Than Bugs?

You must enjoy the outdoors, or pretend that you do. When you hike into bear country, be sure to take someone along who runs slower than you do.

Chapter 6: Entertaining Visitors 62
Or, If That's Mom and Dad, It Must Be Summer

They want to see Mount McKinley and go fishing. But keep in mind if they visit you in summer, you can visit them in winter. So, cultivate friends in warm places.

Chapter 7: Entertaining Strangers 68
Or, What to Do with Frozen Freeloaders

A few ways to get rid of a guest who is stretching your hospitality: Talk religion. Practice a musical instrument, preferably the bagpipes. Sing John Denver's greatest hits.

Chapter 8: Entertaining Friends 74
Or, How to Survive the Party

You know it's time to go when the host waves a shotgun in the air. It is perfectly OK to leave through a window, especially if you have been messing with someone else's woman.

Chapter 9: How to Celebrate the Holidays 86
Or, If the Sun's in Your Eyes, How Can You See the Fireworks?

Memorial Day signals the start of serious fishing, Labor Day means it's time to hunt, and if you're having a mid-life crisis, spend a holiday on Mount McKinley.

Chapter 10: Alaska Courtship 92

Or, the Odds Are Good,
but the Goods Are Odd

The biggest challenge of starting a new relationship is to figure out how to conceal your true personality. And don't take your new love snow machining too soon.

Chapter 11: Living Together 100

Or, Must Your Relationship Degenerate into Marriage?

Know when to argue. Be careful what you say. Know when to give up. And if all else fails, you can just go out for a pack of cigarettes and never come back.

Chapter 12: Time to Have Kids 110

Or, What To Do When Your Biological Clock Goes Off

Sell off his gear. Turn the wanigan into a nursery. Go to child-birth classes. And keep in mind, labor pains most likely will begin in the middle of a cold, dark night.

Chapter 13: Bringing Up Baby 120

Or, Tips for Saving Your Slim Whitman Records

Invite both grandmothers, and put them to work. When bundling up the baby for an outdoor winter outing, remember, there is no such thing as too many clothes.

Chapter 14: The Mother's Curse. 128

Or, Yipes, They've Become Teenagers !

How to deal with the trauma: Send them away or lock them in a closet until they are eighteen. Your goal is not to make their teen years enjoyable. It is to make them survivable.

Chapter 15: Divorce and Remarriage 138
Or, Adding Insult to Injury

Rules to live by: Never be someone's first wife. It ain't cheating if you don't get caught. The wife gets the assets, the husband gets the debts.

Chapter 16: Aging in Alaska 144

Or, Don't Grow Old Gracefully

Age is creeping up on you if: You can't work all day and party all night. You start buying commercial ammo. You lose track of the stories you've told.

Chapter 17: Dying in the Far North 152
Or, If You Can't Go in Style, Why Make the Trip?

Proper behavior for a funeral: Do not show up drunk. Do not hit on the widow. Make sure the deceased is dead.

About the Author 159

Introduction

A new Alaskan is easy to spot. He makes mistakes a *real* Alaskan (anyone who got off the airplane before he did) would never make.

Say he shows up at a Christmas party in Fairbanks wearing a Ralph Lauren shirt, Dockers, and Bass weejuns. He'll pay for this outrageous behavior twice. First, because people will stare and make rude remarks — "What state are you from, pal? Nordstrom?" Second, because he'll soon have the core body temperature of a Popsicle.

Alaska etiquette, you see, is more than a set of rules for high-society brawls. It is a code of conduct suited to surviving on the frontier, where people are more interested in whether you belong to the NRA than the DAR. The code is as intricate as that of civilized places, but it applies to different things. Alaska etiquette is mute about what to do when sitting at a place with seven forks, because the only time an Alaskan puts seven forks on the table is when seven people are eating. But the etiquette for borrowing your neighbor's chain saw, particularly if your neighbor isn't home at the time, is as elaborate as a Japanese tea ceremony.

In Alaska, more than most places, a proper understanding of etiquette depends on a proper understanding of the society. In a region where every other person you meet is likely to be a moody drifter, how important can the rules for proper use of a napkin be? Except, perhaps, those for using it as a tourniquet?

True, parts of Alaska are getting mighty citified — there's a rumor that some people in Anchorage own more neckties than handguns — but most of our 586,000 square miles remains rugged and rural, in attitude if not in fact. So, proper behavior is a lot different in Bethel than in Boston.

This is not the sort of society in which helpful hints from Miss Manners are going to be particularly useful — unless she happens to have hints for escaping from a grizzly bear. But that doesn't mean Alaskans are impolite, or that there is no established code of conduct for frontier life. The purpose of all etiquette is to minimize conflict. In Alaska, where most people are heavily armed, this is a particularly worthy goal. The fundamental principle of Alaska etiquette is this: Any encounter between two or more Alaskans that doesn't end in gunfire is a success.

Alaska etiquette has never been written down until now. Why not? Alaskans can write, can't they? Or at least sign their names? Well, if nothing else, they can make a perfectly legible mark. But Alaskans have such a talent for dispute, even a socially beneficial practice like codifying good behavior can end in an arrest for inciting to riot.

Having to rely on oral tradition is a disadvantage to

newcomers, since often they don't discover their manners are bad until they've displayed them. That can be a humiliating, sometimes painful, experience. So I have decided to help out all the new arrivals — and maybe make a few dollars — by spelling out the best way to act Alaskan.

Consider that Lesson Number One: There's nothing more Alaskan than having an eye for a fast buck.

To adapt to Southeast Alaska, people would have to grow gills. Maybe scales, too. Southeast is *very* wet.

1 Coming Into the Country

Or, Are You Sure This Is a Good Idea?

When I was six or maybe seven, I asked my mother where new Alaskans came from. She hemmed and hawed and told me to go ask my father. He hemmed and hawed and began a rambling tale involving birds and bees.

"No," I said. "Not babies. I already know where babies come from. I learned that in the school yard. I mean new Alaskans."

So, he put me into one of his trucks and drove me out to the Fairbanks International Airport, where we watched passengers getting off Pan American's DC-6 Clipper Ship.

"There," my father said. "New Alaskans."

Even today, most new citizens don't arrive by stork. They come by airplane or boat or automobile, looking for a new beginning.

Or, hoping for a last chance. An Anchorage lawyer once told me he'd figured out the way to make his fortune from the immigrants. He was going to offer an "Alaska Special."

"What's an Alaska Special?" I asked.

"A divorce, a bankruptcy, and a name change," he replied. "All for one low price."

Last I heard, the guy was a millionaire.

Moving to Alaska isn't as simple as pointing the nose of your 1968 Camaro north and flooring it. This is one big place. If, God forbid, California was three times its size, it still would be smaller than Alaska. You could squeeze in Oregon, too. For that matter, all of the United States east of Indiana would fit inside Alaska.

No place this big could be all the same. Just as Florida is much different from Maine, Southeast Alaska is much different from the North Slope. The weather is different. The terrain is different. The lifestyle and customs are different.

Take Southeast Alaska. The area has so little in common with the rest of the state that most Alaskans don't even call it Southeast Alaska. We call it Occupied Canada. Or North Seattle. Some newcomers think that because Southeast is closer to the rest of America, they will be able to adapt more easily. Goes to show what newcomers know.

To adapt to Southeast Alaska, people would have

to grow gills. Maybe scales, too. Southeast is very wet. As a friend says of Ketchikan, which gets more than 200 inches of rain and snow every year: "The air is very clean here because it gets washed so often."

The first rule of living in Southeast is:

Don't wait for the rain to stop.

It won't. If you wait for the rain to stop to go grocery shopping, you'll starve. Buy a yellow rain slicker and some gum boots and just do it. One of the surest ways to identify a Southeasterner is to look at her feet. The gum boots are a dead giveaway. "I bought my first pair of gum boots the other day," a woman once told me. "I felt like I'd married the place."

Don't complain about the rain.

If you do, everybody will know you're a newcomer. The flip side of the rain rule is:

If the sun shines, drop everything and boogie.

All too often, Southeasteners are stunned by the appearance of the sun. Many run and hide, shouting fearfully about "the big yellow thing in the sky." But longtime residents know the proper response to sunshine is to get out in it. For example, any sunny day in Juneau, the state capital, automatically becomes a Sun Day. State employees stream out of their offices, untie their yachts, and go for a sail. The rest of the state never notices, because state employees get just as much work done as any other group of public employees. Nothing.

So, if you happen to be in Juneau, do not ask where state employees work. You'll just confuse people.

One other rain-related rule:

Don't say anything about the smell.

All of Southeast Alaska smells like wet wool. Lots of people in Southeast, especially state employees, can afford expensive rain gear. But everyone wears yellow rubber slickers instead. If you've ever worn a yellow rubber slicker, you know it's a no-win situation. If you leave the slicker open, rain soaks your wool sweater. If you zip it up, sweat soaks your wool sweater. Either way, you end up in wet wool. Why wool? In Southeast, it's always chilly enough for a wool sweater.

People who don't like being wet settle farther north. Most end up in Southcentral Alaska. Many settle in Anchorage, which has about half of the state's 600,000 or so residents.

Everybody in Alaska scorns Anchorage. Including most of the people who live there. In *Coming into the Country*, writer John McPhee described the place like this:

> *"Anchorage . . . is virtually unrelated to its environment. It has come in on the wind, an American spore. A large cookie cutter brought down on El Paso could lift something like Anchorage into the air. Anchorage is the northern rim of Trenton, the center of Oxnard, the ocean-blind precincts of Daytona Beach. It is condensed, instant Albuquerque."*

As the place where Alaska and big-city America intersect, Anchorage has some distinctive folkways. In the rest of Alaska, people brag about how they never lock their doors. In Anchorage, people brag about the cost of their home-security systems. Alaskans brag about how often they can see the northern lights. Anchorage dwellers brag about how often they can see the air they breathe. In Alaska, people brag about how often they hear wolves. In Anchorage, people brag about how often they hear gunshots. Alaskans love to talk about how great their state is. About the best Anchorage residents can say of their city is: "Alaska is close by."

This sort of talk has given Anchorage something of a reputation with other Alaskans. Like the fellow who had come into Anchorage from an outlying area.

"How was the trip?" I asked.

"Good," he said. "Not much road construction, not too many motor homes to pass. And when I got to (the Anchorage suburb of) Eagle River, I had time to do what I always do."

"What's that?" I asked.

"Have a Big Mac and load my .45," he said.

Anchorage might be the place most people in Southcentral Alaska live, but Homer is where they'd like to live. Homer is at the end of the road on Kachemak Bay, a little town in a beautiful spot. The population is 50 percent hippies, 50 percent fisher folk, and 100 percent laid back. So laid back, it's horizontal. The town motto is: "If you can't say something groovy about the '60s, don't say anything at all."

True, the fisher folk have to work out on the fishing

grounds. But in port, they like to do as little as possible. Most everybody else acts like they just got back from Woodstock. If you were wondering what happened to that tie-dyed dress you wore thirty years ago, spend a day in Homer. You'll see somebody wearing it, and the odds are fair it'll be a woman.

In Homer, there's no surer way to mark yourself as a visitor than to drive fast or walk fast or talk fast. So, take this advice:

Don't just stop to smell the flowers, stop long enough to see them grow.

If you have to walk two blocks and there's an espresso shop in one of them, you'll be considered odd and antisocial if you don't stop for a double skinny latté.

The other thing that's absolutely required of Homeroids is to brag about where they live. They know most everybody else in Alaska would like to live there, too, if they could figure out how to make a living. The place already has all the potters, painters, and candle-makers it needs. All the deckhands and captains and pilots, too. It has a couple of bakeries, a gourmet res-taurant, and several purveyors of fishing and boating supplies. Last time I looked, it even had a guy who was making a living selling moose-poop swizzle sticks to tourists.

If you don't want to live in the big city, or stand in line to live in Homer, you can always head farther north. Maybe to Fairbanks, the capital of whining about the government and home of fifty-below cold snaps.

Fairbanks is the ice-fog capital of Alaska and the wanigan capital of the world.

In Fairbanks, sophistication means your wool socks match.

Your end tables aren't ammo crates. Your fur hat is dead. Fine dining is eating anything not killed by somebody you know.

Still, the rules of behavior are strictly enforced.

The first rule is:

Don't say anything nice about Anchorage.

Lots of Alaskans merely dislike Anchorage, but Fairbanksans *really* hate the place. They have a terrible inferiority complex about being the second-largest city in Alaska. They are always complaining about how Anchorage is too big for its britches — just because it has a performing arts center and a sports arena and fresh vegetables.

The second rule is:

Don't say anything bad about Fairbanks.

The people who live there know they're not very smart. Why else would they stay in a place where it is winter nine months of the year? Where it gets so cold your car's tires freeze and so does any part of your body that's not covered? By several layers? Where the most exciting thing to do is wait for a new weather forecast. Fairbanksans know all this. And they're afraid that if anybody says it out loud, their neighbors will say, "You know, that's right! I'm leaving." And property values will drop faster than the temperature in January.

The third rule is: Well, there isn't a third rule. You can say and do pretty much anything you want in Fairbanks, and wear anything you want while you're saying and doing it. Just don't try to commit a violent crime. Every citizen is so heavily armed that violent crime in Fairbanks is really a form of Russian roulette. Anything not violent is, of course, not a crime in Fairbanks.

If none of these more-or-less urban places is to your liking, you have two other choices: Road Alaska or Rural Alaska. Some places in each of these large and far-flung subdivisions are colder than others. Some are bigger. They all have different names. But in every other way, they're basically the same.

Road Alaska is a lot like Fairbanks, only without the sophistication. Most places are built around the two mainstays of the Alaska road town — the service station and the roadhouse. You can get gas at one and gassed at the other, and that's about all there is to do there. People who live in Road Alaska don't actually live in these tiny communities. They live near them along all those dirt roads you see trailing off into the woods. They live in everything from big, pricey five-bedroom homes to house trailers, and what they do for a living God only knows.

The basic rules of Road Alaska are: Keep out! No trespassing! This property protected by Smith & Wesson.

People don't move to Road Alaska for the company.

They move there to be left alone. So if you are traveling through Road Alaska, remember:

Be very polite, and keep your hands in plain sight at all times.

The rest of the state, the part without cities and roads, is Rural Alaska. Most of it is pretty darned empty. The basic rule of Rural Alaska is: Don't go there by yourself. Especially in the winter. You could end up dead. And if you don't, it'll only be because the Natives rescued you. Frankly, they're getting a little tired of this. They've been rescuing white people for 250 years, without so much as a thank-you card for their trouble.

If you do go, take everything you'll need. This may be hard to believe, but there's not a single shopping mall in all of Rural Alaska. If you show up without an ax, you're pretty much out of luck. All you can do is hike to the nearest post office, mail in your catalog order, wait for the first barge next year, and hope that your ax isn't still sitting on the dock in Seattle. In the meantime, building that snug little log cabin with your pocket knife isn't going to be easy.

Lots of people think they want to live in Rural Alaska. Some even try. Only a few who aren't born to it last very long. If you turn out to be one of those few, don't be modest about it. A lot of people can say they're from Juneau, Anchorage, Homer, or Fairbanks. But if you can say you're from Eek, you'll gain instant respect from all Alaskans. We'll think you're nuts, but we'll respect you.

Trend-conscious Alaskans decorate with bathtubs and kitchen sinks. Old-timers prefer junked automobiles.

2 | Home Is Where the Heart Is

Or, Creative Use of Dead Animals and Broken Appliances

First-time Alaska renters or house-buyers often comment on the process. Usually, the say something like this: "Holy Hannah! Look at those prices!" That's OK. In Alaska:

Complaining about prices is never bad manners.

There's a time and a place for complaining, though. If you're whining on the telephone to the folks back home, that's perfectly OK. But you might want to think twice about asking the homeowner, "What are you, some kind of blood-sucking pirate?" If nothing else, that might cause the asking price to climb another five grand. How much better to say something like, "It must cause you considerable grief to be forced by the economic system to charge such an exorbitant price." Then, tell the folks back home what a blood-sucking pirate you are dealing with.

People in more civilized places frown on discussions about money. But this is Alaska, a place many people come just for the money. Complaining about the costs is really a form of bragging about how much money you make, since only someone hauling in big dough can afford the prices. For this reason, it is not at all uncommon for people to have the price of their homes printed right on their business cards.

Whether you're renting or buying, however, you should remember that the price you're paying entitles you to ask a lot of nosy questions.

About the neighbors. About the neighborhood. About the personal habits of the owners. Alaskans won't respect you if you don't stick your nose in their business. They'll also take you to the cleaners. Alaska is still frontier enough that if you're not careful, you're likely to be surprised by what you discover in your new neighborhood. When my parents got married in the early 1930s, my father was working in the gold fields north of Fairbanks. After spending the summer with him in a tent, my mother returned to Fairbanks to find a place for winter. She didn't know the town very well, but was able to find a nice little cabin for a reasonable rent. She swept it out, tidied it up, and ignored the odd looks she got from the townspeople. It wasn't until my father came in from the creeks that she learned she had rented a cabin in the town's red-light district.

Red-light districts are no longer so clearly defined, but in Alaska you can easily end up living between an all-night garage and a massage parlor. In fact, I know a guy who built himself a nice home in Sterling, a typical Road Alaska town, only to have his next-door neighbor open a gravel pit.

If you go completely nuts and decide to settle in Rural Alaska, you might think you'll be able to just cut down a few trees and build a cabin. Forget that. In most of Alaska, the trees are so skinny your cabin would look like the second little pig's house of sticks. It would stand up to the wolves about as well, too. Face it, you'll have to import building materials.

Once you have the materials, you have to assemble them into something resembling a dwelling, install heat, find a water source, and so on. In short, you'll have to do a whole bunch of stuff requiring skills. You don't have these skills?

Never admit you can't do everything yourself.

Basically, anyone who moves to Rural Alaska is expected to be a cross between Thomas Edison and Daniel Boone, with a touch of Frank Lloyd Wright thrown in for good measure. And that's just the women. The men are expected to be *really* self-reliant.

You can only tell people you can't do the work if you can do the work.

That's a subtle form of bragging. But if you truly cannot do the work and you admit it, expect sharp criticism. Throughout Rural Alaska, people you've never met will be saying terrible things about you, like "That guy isn't the carpenter he ought to be." Or, "I've seen better Yukon stoves than the one he put in." Such biting personal attacks have driven people right out of Alaska.

The inept have three choices:

1. Keep quiet, do the work the best way you can, and hope no one notices the snow drifting underneath the wall into the living room.

2. Secretly hire some seasoned bush rat to do the work.

3. Haul in an Atco trailer left over from some construction project and pretend that was what you'd planned all along.

The first option is a problem because you could die from exposure. The second is a problem because it is impossible to keep a secret in Rural Alaska, where it is considered good manners to gossip about your neighbors. It shows you care enough to ferret out their deepest secrets and share them with others. So, most inept people pick the third option. Throughout Alaska — not just in rural areas — the Atco trailer is an acceptable solution to any building problem. So, if you run across somebody who has built a replica of Monticello entirely from Atco trailers, the proper response is praise, not criticism.

After you finish drilling a well, digging a drain field, and leveling your trailer, you'll have to furnish your new home. Once, this was easy. Most houses in Alaska contained only two types of furnishings — stuff belonging to dead people and Blazo boxes.

This has changed, of course. Catalogs, chain stores, and warehouse outlets have sprung up all over. Now you can sit on the same purple crushed velour sofa that you left behind in the Lower 48. But if you should happen to be crammed into a tiny rocking chair in an old-fashioned Alaska house, always ask your hostess where she got such wonderful furniture. (Resist the urge to add, "Did you steal it from a family of dwarves?") The question will give your hostess an opportunity to tell you all about her great Aunt Eldusta, recounting in detail just how she died and, if you're lucky, her entire life story as well — provided, that is, Eldusta met her Maker in Alaska. The entire purpose of the story is to allow your hostess to assert her superiority by underscoring how much longer she has been an Alaskan.

Of course, only Natives have been in Alaska very long. Other people come with the booms and go with the busts. Given the perversity of human nature, Alaskans naturally value most what they have least: longevity.

**The longer you've lived here,
the smarter you are.**

As a visitor once put it, "This is the only place I've ever been where all the arguments are settled by who's been here the longest."

So, if Eldusta croaked in the Lower 48, your hostess will redirect your attention to the piano left to her by Herman, her second cousin twice removed, who carried it on his back over the Chilkoot Trail in 1898. You'd be surprised how many large objects got to Alaska that way.

If you find yourself commenting on the numerous Blazo box constructs — they can be used for end tables, bookshelves, pantries, display cases, and dog houses, if the dog is small enough — do not under any circumstances utter the words Blazo box. Instead, compliment your hostess on her clever use of "materials" or skill in arranging "found objects." For those of you who don't know, Blazo is a fire-starting fluid that was widely used in Alaska for decades. As were the boxes. To remind your hostess that her coffee table is four Blazo boxes shoved together is to remind her of her age. And, perhaps, remind her that she has a loaded shotgun next to the front door.

Without bequests from dead relatives and Blazo boxes, you'll have to furnish your trailer in more modern decor. Typically, this means furniture made from entire trees.

A suite of such furniture includes two uncomfortable chairs, one uncomfortable sofa, and three or four rickety tables in various shapes and sizes. If you can't make this furniture yourself, you can buy it at any upscale furniture store for several thousand dollars — more if the bark is still attached.

Far more important than furniture is how you decorate your trailer. Unfortunately, some new arrivals don't seek advice on this point and decorate their new Alaska homes in the same way they decorated their old homes Outside. Soon, they overhear their guests whispering to one another, "Did you see those sad clowns with big eyes? It's like I always say, once an Outsider, always an Outsider."

Another common mistake is decorating in a way you believe is Alaskan, but isn't. More than one new Alaskan has based his home decor on, for example, painted gold pans – not realizing that an Alaskan never displays a painted gold pan anywhere but in the recreation room. A collection looks particularly fine there, arranged on the pine paneling behind the wet bar.

The only true Alaska decorating style is dead animals:

An Alaska home must contain more dead animals than live people.

In a true Alaska home, you hang your coat on a moose-antler rack, sit in a birch-log chair covered with a bear skin, put your feet up on a caribou-antler coffee table, and set your drink on an end table made of endangered owls.

Whatever you do, do not ask where any of the dead animals came from. There's a good chance your host bought it at a garage sale. Regardless, he'll feel obliged to tell you a long, complicated story about how he killed it with his bare hands in the middle of a raging river that he fell into from the top of a high cliff. If he actually killed the damn thing, he'll tell you a story that begins with the history of hunting, includes the exact weight of the bullet, and velocity of the crosswind, if any, and concludes with a recipe for a particularly piquant sauce for moose ribs.

If the dead animal is a bear, his story will include a poem, or perhaps a song, he wrote about how much he respects the animal.

Not all the animal parts used in home decoration have to be identifiable. Take the oosik, for example. Whatever you do, never ask what an oosik is. An oosik is — there's no polite way to say this —the penis bone of a walrus. Because the walrus is well-endowed, an oosik is large enough to make a dandy hiking staff for a Cub Scout. That means anyone who asks about an oosik will be punished by having to listen to some bad jokes.

Once your home is fully festooned with animal body parts, you can turn your attention to the yard. Alaskans invest great time and energy in their yards, so they can enjoy them for the fifteen minutes or so every year they aren't covered with snow.

Any properly decorated Alaska yard must contain the basics:

So, as you plan your yard, include a car on concrete blocks or a used appliance.

If you do not display these things, everyone will know you are a Cheechako.

Lawn ornaments offer the chance to pretend to longevity you don't have. Scrounge around until you find a 1948 DeSoto. Haul it to your house and mount it on blocks. Visitors will see it and exclaim, "Wow! A '48 DeSoto. You must be a real sourdough. How do you keep yourself looking so young?"

Then, you can tell them some lie about a facial cream made from duck spit.

The use of broken-down automobiles and appliances as lawn ornaments is a throwback to the days when all of Alaska was rural (often referred to as "the good old days" by people with short memories). The cost of shipping anything north was so high that broken-down automobiles, machinery, and appliances were kept for parts. Because the parts of a 1948 DeSoto would only fit another 1948 DeSoto, the parts were rarely used. By the time anyone figured that out, a decorating school had been established.

Over the years, innovators polished the style. My parents achieved a widely admired effect by allowing the rear end of a 1951 Chevrolet sedan to protrude from their garage. Passersby would stop to comment on how nicely the Chevy kept the garage doors from closing, which gave sightseers a view of the broken furniture and empty boxes.

"What a daring concept," they'd exclaim. "Why, with that rusty wringer-washer in the foreground, you've achieved a fusion of indoor and outdoor space not unlike that found at Versailles."

In Rural and Road Alaska, a broken-down snow machine or four-wheeler is often used in place of a car.

Parts of a light airplane are acceptable substitutes, as are stove-in boats and dead outboard motors.

Recently, a daring new school of yard decoration has turned to the useless plumbing fixture as a replacement for the discarded appliance. Members of the avant-garde are littering their lawns with flower-filled bathtubs and kitchen sinks. This variation is not universally accepted. Members of the old school argue that exchanging the elegant lines of a chest freezer for a squat, blocky toilet is a frivolous insult to an elegant Alaska tradition.

No home-decorating scheme is complete without a wanigan, however, and the more haphazardly placed the better. Wanigans are dandy places to hang moose meat or to work on snow-machine engines, or both. They are so handy and common that many home-decorating consultants argue that you should build one even if you don't need it. This has led to the rule followed in polite society:

Whatever you do, don't forget the wanigan.

In the past twenty-five years, another rule has come into wide acceptance:

Whatever you do, don't forget the satellite dish.

Even if every room in your house is wired for cable, your decorating scheme just won't say Alaska without a satellite dish.

Keep in mind that it takes time to perfect an Alaska house. Even if you have a dead-animal pelt on every flat surface, and *two* wanigans, you have to allow years for patches of fur to fall out of the pelts, and for weeds to crowd out the grass in your front-yard freezer. Like so many things about Alaska, you can't expect to get it right overnight.

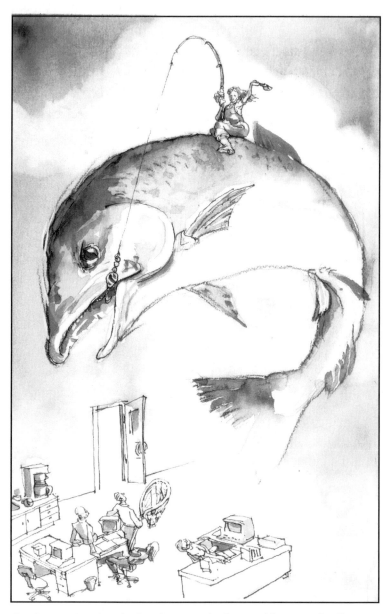

An important rule in the workplace: Never challenge a fish story told by a fellow employee. Just top it.

3 | Finding a Job

Or, How to Compile an Alaska Resume

Don't come to Alaska expecting to have a career. If you are a doctor, a clergyman, or a welfare deadbeat, you might be able to work at one job for your entire life. But everyone else has to take what he can get. A typical Alaska resume — in this case, mine — reads laborer, sign painter, teamster, legislative staffer, campaign consultant, journalist, writer. And mine is pretty stable compared with some.

Never make fun of an Alaskan's resume.

While you're yukking it up about somebody who

got his start running a burger joint, he could be elected governor. But the up side is that you, too, can compile an Alaska resume. The easiest way is to arrive here without a job. Then, like the governor, you can just

Take any job you can get.

A guy I know got his start as a salmon counter. He stood alongside a stream and counted the fish as they swam past on their way to spawn. For this, the federal government paid his room and board, and a salary to boot.

Once you've gotten that first job, work your way up. Remember:

Alaskans admire a self-made man, particularly one who is working with inferior materials.

The friend who started as a salmon counter soon found himself working on a survey crew. From there he clawed his way up to road construction. It seemed the sky was the limit; people were whispering he might someday rise to bulldozer driver. But he made a wrong turn somehow and became a journalist. Not every self-made man finishes the job.

Most newcomers can't find jobs as salmon-counters. So, they have to take jobs with the state's biggest employers: federal, state, or city government. If you're forced to take a government job, don't panic.

You can still find a job with more status.

Frankly, *any* job has more status in Alaska than working for the government.

So, if you find yourself pushing paper for the government, you'll want to get a better job as quickly as you can. Garbage collecting, say, or practicing law. Even lawyers have more status in Alaska than government workers.

If it turns out you can't find other employment,

Do what so many Alaskans do best: nothing.

A few people who do nothing openly admit they are bums, but most have a cover story. Loafers in Road Alaska like to pass themselves off as homesteaders. Many of them actually have broken pieces of homesteading equipment – a chain saw, maybe, or an old flatbed truck with a rusty winch on the front. This junk is usually left out in front of the trailer where people can see it. Mixed in with broken box springs and lengths of pipe, this junk announces to the world that there's homesteading going on.

There's a catch:

In Alaska, nothing can come of homesteading.

The land is not farmable. It is not ranchable. It cannot be made to yield a living. About all a homesteader can do is try to hang on until civilization reaches him and he can get rich by subdividing his land. In Alaska, chances are you'll die first.

If homesteading seems like too much work for you, become a miner. These days, that usually means driving a bulldozer through stream beds, then allowing running water and gravity to do the rest. In addition to being able to make a lot of noise and mess, there's the possibility that you might actually find gold. If you do, you don't have to pay any taxes on it at all. Just put the gold in an old Folgers Coffee can and hide it. Is this beautiful or what?

Saying you're a miner also gives you additional license to complain about the government. Mining is a fine platform from which to whine about stupid EPA regulations, worthless environmentalists, and the commie-liberal Endangered Species Act that prevents you from making a truly tasty owl stew. So,

Never say you are unemployed.
Say you are a miner.

Or, say you are a welder-artist. New public buildings require new public art. Big, new buildings require art on a grand scale. So, the government pays someone to weld together an assortment of junk, put it on a concrete pedestal, and call it art. And people say welfare is a scam.

Figure a couple of hundred bucks for scrap metal and welding rod and the welder-artist turns such a whopping profit that he only needs to slap something together every five years or so. When you see one of these creations (you can't avoid them; they're everywhere), repeat to yourself the official motto of the Welder-Artists Guild: It sure beats working.

However, even after following all this good advice, you might actually have to accept gainful employment and go to work in a real office. If your luck is that bad, this is how you should behave:

Dress like you just got back from checking your trapline.

Coats and ties for men, dresses for women, are out, out, out. Proper Alaska office dress is a flannel shirt, oil-stained jeans, and big, clodhopper boots. North of the Alaska Range, an outer layer of lined coveralls is required. In Southeast, of course, the chic outer layer is a yellow, rubber slicker.

Men usually complete this ensemble with a greasy bill cap from a heavy equipment company.

A wool shirt can be substituted for flannel. If you are an engineer, you can trade the jeans for khakis. But under no circumstances is a tie allowed in the workplace. And if you wear a coat and tie, your co-workers will assume you're going for a job interview and will begin stealing office supplies from your desk. And that brings us to this important point:

Never sit at your desk.

If you do, your boss might be able to find you. You might have to answer your phone. Someone might stop by to ask a work-related question. But the real reason is, you'll miss out on the team-building opportunities available at the coffee pot.

Never discuss work with your co-workers.

If they were interested in work, they'd be at their desks. Instead, stick to the allowable topics. For men, these include sports, particularly fishing, the weather, and women. For women, these include sports, particularly fishing, the weather, and men. Sharing your insights and feelings on these subjects will bind you to your co-workers and empower all of you to do exactly the same thing the next day.

Never challenge a fish story.

Alaskans regard story-telling about their fishing experiences as entertainment, not occasions for truth-telling. If one of your co-workers tells an exceptionally funny tale about being towed to Seldovia by a 500-pound halibut, do not ask why his forty-pound-test line didn't break. Just nod, laugh, and tell your story about the king salmon the size of a Buick.

Always leave early.

Alaskans will respect this because, by leaving early, you're saying, "I've got more important places to go." In the summer, everyone will assume that's a fishing hole, while in winter your colleagues will surmise you've bought a new snow machine. Just remember, if you leave around 3:30 p.m., there's a risk you'll run into your boss on her way back from lunch.

Like any workplace, an Alaska office can be a place of complex, idiosyncratic ritual. But these rules are a solid foundation for survival. They will help you even if you happen to do blue-collar work. Just remember to add a battered Thermos to the work ensemble, curse more frequently, and show off your latest tattoo.

It is impossible for an Alaskan to have too many dogs. In Rural Alaska, these dogs must be huskies.

4 | An Alaskan Is as an Alaskan Does

Or, How to Become Rude, Crude, and Well-Equipped

What does it take to become an Alaskan? Newcomers are often confused about this, because, basically, newcomers aren't very smart. Lucky for them, blending into Alaskan society is simple. It has to be, considering the people who want to do it.

The first step is to develop an Alaska attitude. After all, you're more Alaskan than anyone who arrived on a later airplane. So flaunt it.

What is an Alaska attitude? Basically, it's a Texas attitude without the humility. So assert yourself. Make your opinion known. Tell people what's what and who's who. If somebody tells a story about being chased up a tree by a bear, you tell a story about chasing a bear up a tree. If somebody says earthquakes are the result of plate tectonics, you say they're the result of experiments by the Mole People. If somebody challenges something you say, you challenge him by saying, "Oh yeah, how long have you lived here?"

Of course, if his answer is that he's lived here longer than you have, change tactics. Do what an Alaskan would do: lie. Try to make your lie believable. I got into an argument with one of my pals in high school, and he tried to win by insisting he'd lived here forty years.

"But you're only fifteen," I said. That hardly made him pause.

"Well, the first twenty-five years were in another life," he said.

You don't have to know everything.
In fact, you don't have to know anything.

But there are certain subjects you have to master, or *pretend* to have mastered.

You have to:

Complain about the government. Once, it was enough to have ordinary complaints, about the Internal Revenue Service, say, or about whoever happened to be president. Over the years, however, complaining about the government has become a specialty every bit as complex as low-temperature physics. If you can't find a way to include black helicopters, the cover-up of alien abductions, and NAFTA in your complaints, you haven't got a chance in most Alaska social settings.

Complain about the weather. If it's sunny, complain about the heat. If it's chilly, complain about the cold. If it snows, complain about the snow. If it doesn't snow, complain about the lack of snow. (If you live in Southeast, of course, all you have to do is complain about the rain. That's all it does there.) No matter what the weather is doing, don't forget that it reminds you of a time when it was doing more of it. Or less of it. Or about the same amount, but you were trying to fly a small airplane with a balky engine through it.

Complain about newcomers. Nobody likes 'em. They're just cluttering up the place, destroying the frontier lifestyle, scaring the wildlife, and making it more difficult to find bears to chase up trees. If you are a newcomer, or the people you are complaining to are, be nimble.

Complain about tourists. Alaskans are tired of tourists filling up their campgrounds, tramping through their salmon streams, and jamming their roads with large recreational vehicles so slow that the Alaskans, who are by-God citizens of this great state, can't drive any faster than the speed limit. We all think tourists should give us a break, and just mail us their money.

Praise anything Alaskan. The people who live in Alaska can't get enough of hearing nice things about their state. Remind everyone that Alaska is the biggest state in the union, with the tallest mountains and the feistiest salmon. But don't stop there. Our weather is the coldest, our rainstorms are the wettest, and our clearcuts are the ugliest, too. And when it comes to politicians, no state has any more ignorant or crooked than Alaska's.

Once you've got your attitude down pat, it's time to

work on displaying all the signs and symbols of a *real* Alaskan.

Start a feud with a neighbor. The feud doesn't have to be about anything in particular. Political differences will do, but Alaskans who take pride in their feuding favor some slight, either real or imagined, or a convoluted business deal gone bad. Best of all, of course, is a dispute over a property line.

One of the most important, and most overlooked, facets of a well-conducted feud is its pace. Some people — particularly newcomers anxious to show how Alaskan they are — use firepower much too early. Never begin a feud with gunfire. Your neighbors get more entertainment value from a feud that begins with hard words, progresses through fisticuffs and, perhaps, a few dog shootings, then reaches a shoot-out. If you *begin* with the shoot-out, and either you or your neighbor is a good shot, the feud ends practically before it's begun. What fun is that?

Fortify your home. Some experts on Alaska etiquette insist you should take this precaution *before* engaging in a feud. Most Alaskans would consider such a step to be proof that you are the sort of lowlife who would actually show up at a shoot-out sober. Besides, there are other reasons to fortify your home. You may have to defend yourself in case the government sends troops to collect your back child support.

Collect dogs. One of the things an Alaskan cannot have too many of is dogs. In Rural Alaska, etiquette requires that these dogs be some sort of husky. In Road Alaska, the dogs can be huskies, or any of the dozen or so psycho-killer breeds like pit bulls, Rottweilers, or Slabovian Face-Eaters. In the urban part of the state, they can be almost anything, even little yappy dogs that need frequent shampooing. You need enough dogs to consume anyone who tries to take any of your stuff, or at least whip up such a storm of fierce yipping that the intruder is rendered helpless with laughter. And enough to sustain the dog-shooting stage of your feud. Few things are more embarrassing than running out of dogs in mid-feud.

Collect guns. This is another of the things Alaskans can't have too many of. Even if you happen to collect one gun of every caliber known to man, you can't stop there. A *real* Alaskan's gun collection has one of every make and caliber, including several illegal automatic weapons that only your closest couple of hundred pals in the NRA are privileged to see. Alaskans with monster gun collections claim they are for self defense or for hunting, but we all know what Freud would say about this. He'd say, "Damn, is that a water-cooled, .30-caliber machine gun? You are a *real* Alaskan, aren't you?"

Now that you have everything necessary to survive the Third World War, or maybe to start it, you have to Alaskanize your wardrobe. As we've already seen, you'll need flannel shirts and jeans for your working wardrobe. But what about casual wear? And formal wear? Simple.

Casual wear is just work clothes you've spilled battery acid on.

Unless you spill too much, in which case you suddenly find yourself naked. But if you just spill a little battery acid, your flannel shirts and jeans will develop little holes that grow with every washing. This kind of casual wear doesn't just say, "Hey, I'm an Alaskan." It says, "Hey, I'm the kind of rough, tough Alaskan who carries car batteries around." Of course, it also says, "Hey, I'm clumsy," but you can't have everything.

In Alaska, there's no such thing as formal wear.

If Alaskans wanted to wear fancy dress, they would never have left sophisticated places like Boise, Idaho and Chico, California. True, you'll occasionally see an Alaskan in a lime green leisure suit worn over one of those shirts that looks like it was made from a pinto pony, but that's about as formal as anybody here gets. Unless you count the Alaska Tuxedo.

The Alaska Tuxedo is a wool suit, usually gray or light green, worn with a wash-and-wear or flannel shirt and a bolo tie.

An Alaska Tuxedo can be worn anywhere.

At weddings, funerals, or bar mitzvahs; it's never out of place. In fact, many Alaskans believe the Alaska Tuxedo is the only appropriate outfit for a corpse. So that when you have to prop the deceased against a wall at the wake to make room for dancing, he'll look like just another one of the old-timers who has had too much to drink.

Although Alaska casual and work clothing is unisex, there's a continuing dispute about whether the Alaska Tuxedo is appropriate formal dress for women. Some fashion arbiters maintain that, in formal situations, women should wear skirts. Most women pay no attention to this advice, since it's not the fashion arbiters who might have to hike home from a party when the Weasel breaks down at fifty-below. A few of the more easily influenced women can be seen at galas actually wearing skirts, but they keep insulated coveralls in the Weasel for the trip home.

Once you're acting and dressing like an Alaskan, you have to learn how to speak like one. Until recently, that wasn't easy. Although much of what Alaskans say sounds a lot like English, we have our own words and expressions, and our own meanings for other words you might actually think you recognize. All of this made it tough for a newcomer to speak like an Alaskan. But then a clear-thinking and far-sighted Alaskan — that's me, a real humanitarian — wrote a book that allowed even the newest Cheechako to speak Alaskan right off. So, if you want to avoid any spoken faux pas, buy *How to Speak Alaskan.* By a happy coincidence, it's available from this very publisher for the modest price of $4.95.

You'll be speaking the language in no time. Then, you begin accumulating *stuff*.

As we've already seen, broken stuff is the key ingredient in decorating home exteriors. But stuff is important in other ways.

An Alaskan's standing is largely determined by how much stuff he owns.

This keen social awareness is particularly prevalent in Rural Alaska, where a guy with three broken outboard motors might be able to make them into one working outboard. Or, at least sell you one of those tricky little throttle springs that leap into the water at every opportunity, leaving you to paddle a boat full of gear back home against the current with nothing better for a paddle than a haunch of freshly killed moose.

You can never have too much stuff.

If you come into a little extra money, buy yourself another four-wheeler. Even if you already have a half-dozen of them. Your neighbors will look at you funny if you don't. Besides, everybody knows the odds against any particular four-wheeler running for more than a couple of days in a row. If you already have a four-wheeler for every day of the week — the acceptable minimum number — buy something else. Whatever you do, do not give in to your spouse's plea that the kids need shoes. What do the kids need shoes for? They can drive the four-wheelers. Instead, buy a new rifle, or make a down payment on another boat.

In urban Alaska, the stuff you can own with a straight face is more limited. Since you can get parts and professional repairs, owning more than three four-wheelers might be considered eccentric. But that doesn't mean you have to fritter away your hard-earned money on health care or retirement funds. It's not considered at all odd to own absolutely the best and most expensive stuff. And to complain that even more costly stuff isn't available. So don't be afraid to wail: If only Saab made a pickup!

Some urbanites purchase only enough stuff to avoid being run out of their neighborhoods. They save their money for more important things. *Gear.*

There is still considerable debate among Alaskans over exactly where to draw the line between stuff and gear. Stuff tends to be heavy and motorized. Gear more mobile and muscle powered. But the advance of technology is blurring these lines. A skiff with an outboard is definitely stuff. A canoe is absolutely gear. But an inflatable raft with an outboard? Answering that question can keep things interesting at the office coffee pot for weeks.

You can never have too much gear.

Innovation makes whatever you just bought obsolete practically overnight. If you shell out $1,200 for a fiberglass canoe, the following week someone will unveil a lighter, stronger, and more expensive canoe made of Kevlar. Buy a lightweight nylon backpacking tent, and before it starts to mildew you'll be able to get a lighter one, hand-woven from the breath of angels, for only twice the price. If a piece of gear is new, you have to buy it. Even if you have a slightly older piece of the same gear with the pricetag still on it.

This makes the outdoor show one of the season's most important social events. If you aren't seen at a large show, paying a nose-bleed price for a new, matte-black ninja hatchet, you just aren't anybody. Spouses have been known to lock their gearheads up during show season, after first closing the bank accounts and feeding the credit cards to the dogs.

No matter what they do, it doesn't work. Gear collecting, like stuff collecting, is a game with only one rule: He who has the most when he dies, wins. And no *real* Alaskan wants to be a loser.

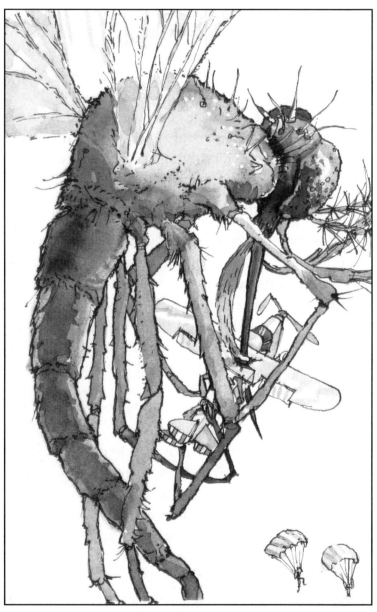

The bugs in Alaska are more likely to relieve you of several quarts of blood than are the bears.

5 | Surviving the Outdoors

Or, Are Tourists Worse Than Bugs?

Once you have an Alaska-sized portion of stuff and gear, there's no way to avoid going outdoors. To live in Alaska:

**You must enjoy the outdoors.
Or, pretend that you do.**

Why? Simple. People have to justify moving this far north, somehow, and many do not want to admit the truth: They're just here for the money. So, love of the outdoors is a handy cover story, because what Alaska has the most of is outdoors. If you believe people forced to go to the bathroom in the bushes are going to let you get away with staying in the city, think again.

So, you might say, what's the big deal? I'll just lie.

Lying is the proper way to handle many social situations.

Don't believe me? Ask yourself this: If you're going out to dinner with your wife's family, and your mother-in-law asks how she looks, what do you say? Do you tell the truth, which is: "I've seen better-looking bus wrecks?" Or, do you say, "Wonderful," thereby saving the evening and, probably, your marriage? You lie, of course. Everybody does it.

Unfortunately, the risk of getting caught in an outdoor lie is high. Good manners require that when telling an outdoor story, you must answer every question you're asked. And there are so many details to the simplest outdoor story that even the most careful liar is bound to get tripped up.

Say you're standing around the coffee pot, listening to a detailed discussion of monofilament fishing line, and a co-worker asks what you did over the weekend. The truth is, you spent the weekend at home, listening to opera and drinking wine so fancy the bottle had a cork. Are you going to tell your co-worker that? Particularly if he's the guy who once told you about being forced to strangle a grizzly bear with his bare hands? Heck, no. You're going to lie. You're going to say, "fishing."

"Whereabouts?" he'll ask.

"Oh, on the Kenai," you'll say.

"Whereabouts on the Kenai?" somebody else will ask.

You might just as well give up right there. If your co-workers ask more than one question, they'll keep asking until you stick your foot in your mouth. Even the most carefully contrived cover story is no match for Alaskans' ability to ask questions about geography, weather, and gear. Pretty soon, somebody will ask, "What color did you say that Pixie was again?" And you're a done duck.

So, if you want to have any friends, you're going to have to go outdoors.

You're going to have to pack a bunch of gear, maybe load it into a Weasel or some other big piece of stuff, and head for the boonies. And you're not going to be able to just Weasel around for the weekend, either. When you are outdoors, you actually have to do something.

What you have to do depends on where you are. If you live in Rural or Road Alaska, you have to destroy something. That something can be trees, cut down for logs or firewood, or a stream, bulldozed while mining. But it's far better if the something has some chance, however remote, of eluding you. That, after all, is why fishing and hunting are considered sports, even though the sport involved in four-wheeling up to an unarmed moose and shooting it with a large-caliber weapon is difficult for some people to see. No other outdoor activity is considered as manly as killing *something*. Besides, if you live far enough from a supermarket, you might need to eat it.

If you live in the city, you are not absolutely required to destroy something.

You can simply go for a hike, ride a mountain bike, or pitch a tent. But people who don't at least try to destroy something are suspected of having environmental leanings. And, in Alaska,

The only good environmentalist is an environmentalist in California, where she belongs.

No matter why you go outdoors, you'll find it's full of dangers. Different people see different dangers. For example, I fear few things as much as being forced to eat freeze-dried food. But some people, particularly visitors and new Alaskans, are most afraid of bears.

They shouldn't be. The fact is, bears rarely eat entire people. Oh, a grizzly might taste a camper now and then. And if you happen to be carrying fresh salmon, a bear will mug you for them. But, as a foodstuff, people are stringy and, apparently, not very tasty to your average bear. So, in most cases, if you are polite to the bear, the bear will be polite to you. In this context, "polite" means giving the bear whatever it wants, including your cash card and personal identification number. You can always get a new PIN. New arms and legs are harder to come by.

Now, so-called experts will give you lots of confusing advice about what to do if you encounter a bear. You're supposed to do one thing if the bear is black, another if it's brown. Great advice, except that some black bears are brown and some brown bears are black. Not to mention all the bears out there that are cinnamon, beige, or cordovan. Or, for all I know, some trendy new shade. Humus, maybe, or anthracite. The only dependable way to handle bears is to do what I do:

When hiking into bear country, always take along somebody who runs slower than you do.

Actually, bugs are far more likely to relieve you of a couple of quarts of blood than bears are. Some people claim the twin-engine mosquito is the worst of the bugs, but I say they can be dealt with, as long as shoulder-mounted surface-to-air missiles continue to be available on the black market. Other people nominate the white sock, a biting fly that takes flesh as well as blood. Still others claim the worst insect is the blood-sucking politician. Like many Alaskan debates, this one will never be resolved. Let's just say that there are plenty of ferocious bugs outdoors. So, never ask a co-worker what happened to his face. If he didn't fall head-first into a pile of porcupines, he made the Cheechako mistake of going fishing with a bug spray the insects thought was meat tenderizer.

Another outdoor horror is tourists. There are two distinct types of horrible tourists. Type One is the motor-home driver, whose age is directly proportional to the size of his vehicle. The older the driver, the bigger the rig. Thus, an old geezer with lousy reflexes will be piloting the forty-footer down the highway at forty mph. Probably with an equally old geezerette telling him he's driving too fast. The only way to keep a weekend outing from taking a week is to pass every motor home you see.

Type Two is the tourist you find in your favorite fishing spot. He will be very irritating. For one thing, he'll probably have better gear than you do. For another, he's more likely to speak German than English. For a third, he'll no doubt be rude and pushy. Little does he know that, in such situations, Alaskans are honor-bound to prove nobody can be ruder or pushier than an Alaskan. Even if you hate to fish, you're required to crowd right in on the guy, explaining in a loud voice that this is your fishing hole, and no by-God foreigner is going to run you off of it. If he says something foreign in return, deal with him the Alaska way. Talk louder. It's a well-known fact that even the dimmest foreigner will understand English once you get into the ninety-decibel range.

No wonder the scariest thing in the Alaska woods is an Alaskan. He'll spook your fish, scare your game, and destroy your sleep. If you're out for a hike, he'll scare the bejabbers out of you by barreling past on his mountain bike. If you're biking, his four-wheeler will run you off the trail. And there's nothing worse than a head-on between two Weasels. Even if no one is seriously injured, it'll take days to sort out all the gear.

In the summer, you just have to put up with this. As an Alaskan, remember:

You can take a vacation in the summer, but you can't leave the state.

Doing so is considered very bad manners. So, all you can do is keep an eye peeled for your fellow citizens. And if your walking stick should accidentally become tangled in the spokes of their mountain bike wheels, well, they have to look out for their fellow citizens, too.

All this is very well in the spring and summer, when having to dive into the devil's club is about the worst damage other outdoor recreationists can inflict. And nobody goes ten feet from a road in the fall, because that's hunting season. You'd be surprised how many things look like a moose to an Alaska hunter, including another hunter dressed from head to toe in alert orange. Think how poor your chances would be if you didn't have a gun of your own to shoot back with.

Yet, even going for a walk in the fall in a moose suit is smarter than going outdoors in the winter. It's cold in the winter. And dark. And, in most of the state, it's snowy, too. All good reasons to stay indoors and conduct a scientific taste test of various barley- and hops-based beverages.

Many people do go outdoors in the winter. They ski. They skate. They drive snow machines. They mush dogs. They think it makes them *real* Alaskans. How wrong they are.

In winter, real Alaskans do not go outdoors. Real Alaskans go to Hawaii.

Darn near anything will impress your visitors. A structure built before 1930 qualifies as historical.

6 | Entertaining Visitors

Or, If That's Mom and Dad,
It Must Be Summer

One of the best things about moving to Alaska is escaping your past. A *real* Alaskan is happy to have Canada between himself and his parents. Or, himself and his ex-wife. Or, himself and the parents of that girl down the street who sure looked eighteen.

Unfortunately, Alaska is not far enough away to discourage visitors. For that, you'd need to move at least as far away as Pluto. Still, it could be worse.

Nobody ever visits Alaska in the winter.

Depending on which part of the state you live in, you've got anywhere from six to nine months to yourself. No freeloading relatives. No former college friends who need to be chauffeured around. No Congressional delegations on fact-finding trips.

Unfortunately, that leaves several vulnerable months. And, unless you're prepared to send death notices to your family each and every May, you're going to have to show visitors around. And pretend you're enjoying it. Fortunately, if you remember a few simple rules, the experience doesn't have to be any worse than a bad head cold.

First, remember they are outsiders. Darn near anything will impress them. I've had a lot of luck passing off ordinary ice cubes as chunks of glacier. I have drawn "oohs" and "aahs" by pointing out that you can see right through the air here. I have claimed – without contradiction – that various neighborhood dogs were famous leaders of Iditarod racing teams, and I once convinced a particularly dim acquaintance that the local utility substation was the source of the northern lights.

"Yup," I told him, "they just throw a switch and the old aurora starts to dance."

The fact is, people come to Alaska expecting the unusual. Apparently, they are unaware that all they have to do to find it is to stop into the first Alaska bar they see. This quest allows some Alaskans to make a fine living taking visitors to drive-up glaciers, showing them big vegetables, and pointing out buildings from the 1930s, which qualify as historic in Alaska. Sometimes, if the visitors are from a foreign country, the search for bizarre Alaska sights takes them to *very* strange places indeed.

Like my neighborhood. I live in an old subdivision in Anchorage, built in the early 1960s so that oil company office workers who came north could move into split-level houses just like the ones they'd left behind. It's a nice neighborhood, but nothing special. If it was special, would they let me live there? Still, every once in a while, a bus pulls up in front of my house and disgorges thirty or forty Japanese people with cameras. They proceed to walk through the subdivision, looking where their tour guide points and taking pictures.

I am not making this up.

What could the tour guide be telling them?

"This is the typical dwelling of an overpaid, underworked Alaskan, who has 2.4 children who don't study much and spend all of their free time watching television and hanging out in malls. On weekends, the air is thick with smoke from the ritual incineration of meat, in a ceremony known as the Bar-B-Q."

What do you suppose the tourists are going to do with all those snapshots of my crabgrass? The videotape of a Twinkies wrapper blowing through my dandelions? I have this mental image of some couple in Osaka showing the footage to their friends and saying, "This Alaska. What a primitive place. Look what an atrocious gardener this guy is. No wonder these people have to drive Hondas."

Second, remember they are Outsiders. All they want to do is see Mount McKinley and fish. Don't tell them the nation's highest mountain is mostly obscured by clouds. Take them to the park. They may not get to see the mountain, but they'll be impressed by all the motor homes with out-of-state plates. Besides, what do they know from mountains? Just tell them any nearby peak with snow on it is McKinley. Then take them to the Kenai River, put a pole in their hands, and let them fish. They might not catch anything, but, provided they speak German, they'll be able to swap stories with the other fisher folk.

Third, remember they are Outsiders. Sooner or later, they'll get tired of the long summer days, the gorgeous sights, the amazing wildlife, and all the other great stuff. Then they'll go home. All you have to do is put up with a few salmon bakes, some roadside gold-panning, and stories about how that moose over there reminds Uncle Earl that, back home, the gophers are still wild. Then, you help them pick out some T-shirts and a painted gold pan or two and send them on their way.

And if they don't show signs of going quietly, re-member they are Outsiders. Take them camping. You have all that gear, and it would be a shame to let it go to waste, particularly when there are so many rainy, buggy, and otherwise discouraging places to pitch a tent.

The mosquitoes alone would have Superman look-ing at his watch and saying, "Well, I've got to get back before Perry White blows a gasket." The biting flies would run off the entire Justice League of America. Even your granola-crunching, bunny-hugging, Sierra-Club-bing cousins will remember they left the water running back in Ohio when you're all camped in the middle of nowhere and, at about two a.m., you ask: "Does that sound like one grizzly bear out there? Or two?"

Why should an Alaskan put up with visitors? Well, remember they are Outsiders. During the winter, you might want to go visit *them*. In fact, if they are relatives, and you have children, you *have* to visit them. Sorry, it's a rule. My wife is from California, and practically every trip we take involves showing our kids off to her parents and other relatives. Even today, when the youngest is 19.

"Why, they look just like American children," her relatives say. "I thought you said he was an Alaskan."

Even if they aren't relatives, your visitors incur a debt by mooching off you, a debt that can only be repaid by letting you mooch off them. That's why you must remember:

Cultivate friends in warm places.

Even if you've been lifelong friends with people in Minnesota, dump them. Look for new friends in Arizona or Hawaii. Use the phone book if necessary. Believe me, in mid-December, when it's forty degrees below zero and dark twenty hours a day, you won't be wanting to visit the Swensons in Duluth. You'll be wanting to hang with the Pualoas on the Big Island.

You are expected to help strangers in need, even if you must invite them into your home to do it.

7 | Entertaining Strangers

Or, What to Do with Frozen Freeloaders

Freeloading relatives and fair-weather friends are not the only people Alaskans are required to entertain. There are freeloading neighbors and, under some circumstances, complete strangers, too. Life in Alaska can be a never-ending round of frivolity, food, and drink that you have to pay for.

Take strangers. Under the Frontier Code, you are expected to help those in need, even if you have to invite them into your own home to do it. This provision of the Code is particularly tough for the dead-enders of Road Alaska, who moved out there to escape laws, rules, and unreasonable societal demands, like having to bathe. That's why Road Alaskans keep trying to have this part of the Code repealed, and replaced with something more to their liking. Something like: every man for himself.

So far, though, they haven't been able to muster the votes. So, even if a complete stranger throws himself on your mercy, you're obliged to help. For instance, what if you're sitting in your shack, cabin, or house, and hear a feeble scratching at your door?

Do not fire several rounds through the door, chest high.

Even an Alaska jury will fry your sorry butt if there happens to be a human being on the other side, unless you can prove beyond a reasonable doubt that he was a secular humanist.

So, instead of firing, go to the door and look through the peephole. Imagine you see a frozen human being leaning against your door. Here's what you must do.

Bring him indoors. That's right, into your home. Some people favor flinging open the door and letting him topple into the room, but if he is thoroughly frozen, there is some risk of shattering.

Prop him near the stove. A corner is a good place because there's less of a chance that he will fall over as he thaws. Some etiquette guides recommend putting him right next to the stove, but uneven thawing may leave you with a partially frozen guest.

Give him something warm. Coffee, hot chocolate, and chicken soup are favorites in such situations, although some authorities say there's nothing better than tucking him between a couple of sled dogs. Do not give him hootchinoo. People who get too near the stove with a snootful of hootch tend to explode. Naturally, it's perfectly all right to dose yourself with hootch, as long as you are careful not to exhale in the stove's direction.

Put him in a cold bath. This makes absolutely no sense, but as anybody who has ever thawed a turkey knows, it works. Just don't forget what you're doing and try to pry his giblets out before he's thoroughly thawed. Many experts on frozen people swear by this technique. Its main drawback is that you have to own a bathtub.

Your obligation to this uninvited guest does not end when he is completely thawed. (Most authorities recommend 10 minutes per pound as the average thawing time, but you can tell for sure simply by pinching him in various places.) You also are expected to give him a warm place to sleep, to feed him, and to nurse him back to health.

Don't ask your guest how he happened to become frozen in the first place.

No Alaskan wants to admit he got drunk and drove his snow machine through a hole in the river ice. Or, got drunk, drove his car into a ditch, and tried to walk home from there. Or, got drunk, got sleepy, and decided to lie down on the sidewalk for a nap. (Notice how all these stories involve getting drunk? Most experts agree that if it weren't for booze, there would be hardly any frozen people at all.)

Unfortunately, this social obligation has encouraged some people to feign being frozen as a way to get free room and board. And even among the truly frozen, the soft life of recovery is a powerful inducement to malingering. That's why it is perfectly all right to talk politics with the formerly frozen. A particularly trenchant analysis of the federal government's attempts to cover up the fact that the last four Democratic presidential candidates have been Mole People can make someone with no feeling at all in his hands and feet leap out of bed and sprint right out of your cabin.

There are, of course, many other socially acceptable ways to hurry a guest toward renewed health.

Talk religion. Especially good is a detailed description of Satanic sacrificial rites you participate in regularly.

Practice a musical instrument. Playing the first sixteen bars of *Stairway to Heaven* over and over has actually restored the hearing of people thought deaf, particularly when you play it on the bagpipes.

Sing John Denver's greatest hits. *Annie's Song* alone has cured more fake paralysis than Jimmy Swaggert. But don't overdo it. Playing a recording of John Denver singing John Denver's greatest hits is considered unacceptable behavior, even if you're sure the guy eating you out of house and home wasn't even seriously cold, let alone frozen. Besides, playing this music is a Class C felony in many parts of the state.

The Frontier Code's injunction to help strangers is so strong that Alaskans must follow it even when they are not home. If you happen to live in a remote cabin, for example, you are expected to leave food, water, and fuel in the cabin, and leave the latchstring out. To those of you from more civilized areas, this might seem like asking for it. But remember: The Frontier Code does not specify what sort of food you have to leave, or how much fuel. A few days of eating Rodent Helper and having to cut his own wood will cause even the laziest old coot to depart for better accommodations.

Like many rules of Alaska etiquette, the requirement to help strangers arises from the nature of the place. Alaska is a difficult, sometimes dangerous, place to live, and most everybody will need help now and then. The person you help today may help you tomorrow. So Alaskans are a pretty tolerant lot, and it's hard to make them so mad they won't help you.

Hard, but not impossible. Here, in a story told by my friend Mike Carey, is an example.

One evening, Austin E. "Cap" Lathrop, Fairbanks's leading citizen in the 1940s, was leaving a cafe when he bumped into three Cheechakos. He asked them what they thought of Alaska. One thought the place was great. The second thought it was OK. The third was scornful, saying many things that reflected badly on the Territory and the character of its citizens.

Cap asked the three if they'd found work yet. They all said no.

"In that case," Cap said, "you and you" — he pointed to the first two men — "come down to my office first thing in the morning and I'll put you to work."

Then he pointed to the third man.

"And you," he said, "I suggest you get the hell out of here on the next boat or train. Alaska doesn't need people like you."

Never try to manage an Alaska party. You might as well try to manage an avalanche. Let it happen.

8 | Entertaining Friends

Or, How to Survive the Party

Let's say you're tired of having a nice house, friendly neighbors, and cordial relations with the local police. Throw a party. After your friends break all your windows playing Ultimate Frisbee in the living room, after your neighbors get tired of listening to *Shake Yer Booty* played over and over at top volume, after the police arrive at your house for the fifth time to find everybody who hasn't passed out playing naked Twister, your house will be in ruins, you'll be at odds with the neighbors and on the wrong side of the law. In other words, you'll be an Alaskan.

How do you get a bunch of people to come over to

eat your food, drink your liquor, and get cherry-flavored body lotion all over your Barcalounger? Just ask.

As you might expect, Alaskans tend toward informal invitations. An occasion that, in Peoria, might require engraved invitations and hand-written responses, is settled face to face in Alaska.

Inviter: Want to come over to the house Saturday and get soused?

Invitee: Sure, if I've got the Weasel running by then.

The rule is simple:

When inviting someone to your house, don't be formal.

That can cause trouble. If you live alone, showing up at home with five or six people isn't much of a problem. As long as you've got plenty to drink, and one of you is sober enough to heat some pizza rolls, your party will be fine. But if you have an unsuspecting spouse, things can turn ugly particularly if a significant percentage of the people you bring home are good-looking members of the opposite sex. In cases like this, Alaska etiquette demands that the spouse stick to blunt instruments. Pots and pans, thrown or swung, are fine. So are rolling pins — if they even make such things anymore — and baseball bats weighing less than thirty-two ounces.

Sharp-edged weapons and firearms are prohibited.

Look at it this way. If you shoot your spouse for

bringing home uninvited guests, how can you top that if you catch him or her chippying around?

For this, and other reasons, modern manners mavens generally advise you to include your spouse in your social plans. Let him or her know that everybody within a fifty-mile radius is eating and drinking at your house on Friday night. You'll be happier. Your spouse will be happier. And your health-insurance carrier will be happier, too.

I've actually received elegantly written cards that say things like: "Come on over and put on the feedbag. We'll be dancing 'til we puke later." Sending such invites is generally regarded as putting on airs. The only excuse for a written invitation is if you are having a serious blowout and need to make photocopies to post on telephone poles, trees, and the post office bulletin board.

An often overlooked advantage of planning a party in advance is that it gives you time to hide the breakables. This is in no way considered an insult to your guests. In fact, exactly the opposite is true. If you leave out that collection of Hummel figurines, it's a message to your guests that you doubt their ability to get rowdy.

The first rule of entertaining at home is:

You can never have too much to drink.

There's a lot of talk about alcohol problems these days, but most Alaskans believe the only alcohol problem is not having enough. The general rule of thumb is that, for every couple invited, you should have on hand a case of beer and a couple of screw top jugs of wine. For large gatherings, double this estimate. Once the word gets out you're throwing a party, people will snow machine in from all over. Of all the social gaffes you can make as a host or hostess, there is nothing worse than running out of drinks.

Not to worry. In Alaska, you can make your own alcohol. In parts of Rural and Road Alaska, in fact, it is expected that you will have on hand a supply of home-brewed beer or hootchinoo. There is a lot of literature available on home brewing, so mixing hops, barley, water, and yeast in proper amounts should be child's play. Although children should be limited to brewing 3.2 beer.

Much less is known about making hootchinoo, or hootch for short. Frankly, that's as it should be. Hootch is as explosive as rocket fuel and twice as unstable. Not to mention three or four times more potent. Old-timers call it "40-rod whiskey" because it can kill you from that distance. Amateurs really should not make the stuff. Or, drink it for that matter. But since you might be desperate sometime, I'm including instructions for the preparation of hootch:

Recipe for Hootch

Fill a stout container three-fourths full of water. Add canned fruit of some sort, the more cans the better. Mix thoroughly. Add sugar. Seal container. Wait.

Do your waiting at a distance, and make sure that you are using a dwelling you don't care anything about. Hootchinoo explosions have killed more miners than consumption and destroyed more log cabins than carpenter ants.

After a proper period (some experts recommend as long as a week), open the container and taste. If your hair doesn't fall out within twenty-four hours, the hootch is ready to drink.

You'll notice that some of the instructions are not precise. That's because making hootch is an individualistic process. And because survivors of the hootch-making process guard their recipes jealously. So, you might want to consider sticking to beer brewing. Beer rarely explodes.

Once you have your liquids lined up, you can turn your attention to solids. Parties where only liquor is served end too fast. Everyone passes out before anyone can do anything even remotely scandalous. And any party that doesn't end in at least one divorce is considered a failure. So, you need some food to blot up the booze. If you are tempted to begin with fancy appetizers, don't.

Begin by having your guests check their firearms at the door.

Otherwise, before the evening's over, somebody is going to want to prove she can shoot the earrings off the bimbo wrapped around her husband. If anyone objects to surrendering their weapons, remind them that when it comes time for party games, "Strip Searching the Suspect" is always popular.

Alaskans look on crab puffs, tofu finger food, and duck-sausage pizza as the sort of foreign kickshaws intended to thin good, red American blood and turn us all into slaves of the United Nations. For an Alaska party, don't make anything elaborate. People will wonder if you're a secret agent of Boutros Boutros-Ghali and the New World Order. (Sounds like a rock band, doesn't it?)

Play it safe. Just spread some chips around. Leave them in the bags. If you want your appetizers to say "upscale," include a few jars of salsa.

If you must make something, you can never go wrong with Spam. Here is a recipe for the perfect Alaska appetizer:

> Take a piece of Sailor Boy pilot bread. Break into chunks. On each chunk, place a hunk of Spam. On top of the Spam, place of chunk of canned pineapple. Jam a plastic toothpick through the whole thing. Serve.

These chunk-hunk-chunk appetizers are sure to be a hit, served as the centerpiece of an all-appetizer party or as a prelude to a sit-down dinner. Some innovators have tried various substitutions and, in fact, during the late 1970s, canned corned beef enjoyed considerable popularity. These folks were just trying too hard. Today, the wise host and hostess stick to the original Spam recipe.

You may decide to serve an entire meal. If so, do

not pass up the story-telling opportunities. Your guests will be disappointed if you don't accompany each course with a long, colorful tale about where it came from. Alaskans rarely serve food they will admit they bought at a store, and they don't expect you to admit it, either. The smoked salmon should come with a tale about having to wrestle the fish away from a hungry grizzly. The caribou stew ought to remind you of how the rifle jammed and you had to whack the charging animal on the head with a state hunting regulations booklet. The bread must have been made from sourdough starter directly descended from a batch made by Soapy Smith. And so on.

Your guests will expect you to tell these stories, even if they've seen you take the bread out of the bakery wrapper. It is important to remember:

When telling stories about how Alaskan you are, there's no such thing as lying.

If you say, "Oh, that's stew meat I bought at the market," people are going to stop coming to your soirees.

"She's just too different," they'll tell one another. "Too much of an Outsider."

Once dinner is over — a cobbler made with cranberries you picked on the run while escaping a forest fire makes an excellent dessert — the party starts. For a while, Alaska parties are like parties anywhere: people standing around talking and drinking while music plays in the background. But about the time people at a party in Peoria are saying their good-nights, Alaskans are just getting started.

Never try to manage an Alaska party.

For one thing, it's impossible. You might as well try to manage an avalanche. For another, you might irritate the guests.

"Did he say, 'Let's play Pictionary?'" somebody will shout. "I say, let's pants him!"

The next thing you know, you're locked out of your own house, naked. And the police are pulling up to see who is playing "Shock the Monkey" so loud that the Canadians are complaining.

Just let the party happen.

You'll know that it was a success when one of your friends calls late the next day to ask if you remember what she did the night before. And who did she do it with? And, oh yeah, where did she get this tattoo?

One of the best reasons to throw a party is so that everybody who attends feels obligated to invite you to their parties. If you have a large enough circle of friends, you will have plenty of time to repair the damage to your house before it's your turn again.

The most important rule for a guest is this:

Always bring beer. Never bring guns.

If you follow this rule, you'll be forgiven for most anything else you might say or do.

One thing you should always do is correct the stories told by your host or hostess.

"Wait a minute," you'll say, "the last time you told that story, there were *two* giant grizzlies guarding the fish."

This might cause you to be the last person served cranberry cobbler, but it shows the people throwing the party that you've paid attention to their stories in the past, you care enough to speak up, and you're still sober enough to talk. That will keep them from telling any stories about you.

After dinner, it's perfectly proper to belch.

Not only does this signal the host and hostess that you feel at home, it also can lead to a favorite party game, seeing who can belch the entire *Alaska's Flag Song* the fastest without an unfortunate incident. There are said to be occasions when belching is not appropriate, but I'm darned if I can think of any.

During the party, don't tell tales. This could be dangerous. If you happen to see one of your friends in a dark corner examining the tonsils of a strange woman, don't tell his wife. If you do, she might attempt to do some things that are, at that moment anyway, too taxing for her motor skills. Like unwinding herself from that strange man. Standing up. Searching for her gun. And so on.

After the party, of course, it's perfectly OK to tell tales. Everyone wins. You're the star attraction at the office coffee pot. Your subjects' reputations are enhanced when you say something like, "And you should have seen the expression on that woman's face when Mitzi shot her earrings off." And the social standing of your host and hostess is enhanced by having thrown such a fun-filled party. The best thing about telling tales afterward, of course, is that no one else is likely to remember exactly what happened, so you can say pretty much anything you want.

Perhaps the most difficult thing about going to an Alaska party, besides remembering the next day what you did, is figuring out when the party is over. Some endings are perfectly clear. If they run out of beer, it's time to leave. No Alaskan is expected to try to have a good time while thirsty.

If the host begins brandishing a shotgun, it's time to leave.

You might wish he were being more subtle — and that he had the safety on — but you know perfectly well that if he were, nobody would pay him the slightest attention. If the hostess begins brandishing a shotgun, it's past time to leave. No doubt she has something personal to discuss with the host, like where has he been the past two hours. People are entitled to their privacy. Besides, the shotgun might be loaded with double ought, which has a nasty tendency to spread and take in innocent bystanders. If the party should breakup in this fashion, remember:

There's no shame in leaving through a window.

Many parties lack a clear departure signal, particularly after the host and hostess have given up and gone to bed. Nature is no help. If the party is held in summer, there's no sunrise. The sun never goes down. If it's a wintertime party, the sun never rises. And if you leave too soon, people will call you a short-ball hitter. Few things are more damaging to your reputation than that. Besides,

There's status in being the last to leave.

This combination of circumstances sometimes encourages guests to stay at a party for weeks at a time. This is one answer to the homeless problem. Generally, however, staying longer than two weeks at a party is considered excessive. Unless, of course, there are extenuating circumstances, like bad weather or a particularly good batch of home brew.

If you are throwing the party and your guests refuse to leave after a couple of weeks, duplicity is perfectly acceptable. There are few better endings to an Alaska party than sending your guests out for more Spam, then quickly changing the locks on your doors.

Once the party is over, a guest has one more responsibility. Providing he can remember where the party was, he should thank the host and hostess. Like formal invitations, formal thank-yous are considered too uptown for most Alaskans. A simple telephone call, in which you thank your hostess and ask her if she's seen your girlfriend, will suffice. If you want to be particularly thoughtful, offer to help pay for the damage.

Holidays in Alaska are not like holidays in the Lower 48. You have to learn to make your own fun.

9 | How to Celebrate the Holidays

Or, If the Sun's in Your Eyes,
How Can You See the Fireworks?

Holidays in Alaska aren't like holidays anywhere else.

Take the Fourth of July. Most Alaska communities have fireworks displays, even though it never gets dark. Imagine a crowd of people standing around a baseball field. Something goes bang. The crowd ooohs. A few seconds later, up in the bright summer sky, something goes pop. The crowd ahhhs. After an hour or so of that, everybody goes home.

No matter how hard everyone tries, it just isn't the same as watching a fireworks display somewhere it's dark enough to see the fireworks.

So, throughout Alaska, the holiday rule is:

You have to make your own fun.

On the Fourth of July, this means supplying your own explosions. Fortunately, in Alaska, the material for explosions is always close at hand. Fireworks are illegal in most places, which means they are never in short supply.

Neither are other, even more exciting explosives. When, many years ago, my friends and I decided that an appropriate celebration of the Glorious Fourth would be putting the frame of a 1947 Willys into orbit, we had no trouble finding the dynamite necessary for the launching. True, no piece of the Willys frame got higher than twenty feet off the ground. But, after we'd picked ourselves up and dusted ourselves off, we agreed it had been a marvelous explosion.

If you don't want to go to the trouble of crimping fuses, you can still celebrate the Fourth with a bang. What better time to try out that knee mortar you traded a mining claim for? Or, to sight in your .50-caliber machine gun? Celebrating the Fourth with heavy and/or automatic weapons is a well-established local tradition.

In fact, Alaska is full of local holiday traditions. In Southcentral Alaska:

Memorial Day means it's time to go fishing.

This is true whether you enjoy fishing or not. Every last person is expected to pack up and head for a bay, river, or stream. Which means, of course, that many Southcentral Alaskans celebrate Memorial Day locked in a traffic jam, or removing the hooks of other fisherfolk from various parts of their anatomies.

In interior Alaska:

Labor Day means it's time to go hunting.

Every last person loads a four-wheeler or two onto a trailer, hitches it to the pickup, and drives slowly along the highways, looking for game. If someone sees, say, a moose, everybody stops, unloads their four-wheelers, and races to the moose. Several shots ring out, and the shooters spend the next several hours arguing about whose moose it is. Those who don't get to race, shoot, and argue spend the holiday driving slowly or, if they're really unlucky, dodging lead. People hunting from the saddles of four-wheelers tend to shoot first and identify the carcass later.

Even the locals are smart enough to limit the traditions requiring outdoor activity to the summertime holidays. The rest of the year, if you have family in Alaska, you have to spend holidays with them. Because Alaskans are naturally disputatious, this can lead to elaborate seating arrangements. One Thanksgiving, for example, we had to pass the turkey to one of my uncles, who was feuding with my father, by taxi cab. My mother never did get the platter back.

Then there was the problem with the little kids' table. There were so many people in my family that somebody had to die before you could move up to the adults' table, which, as any little kid knows, is where they keep all the good stuff. That meant some family members were sitting at tiny card tables, eating turkey and stuffing off Snoopy plates well into their thirties.

"You mean I'm old enough to die for my country, but I'm not old enough to sit at the big table?" one of my nephews asked at a recent dinner.

His mother looked up from cutting his meat into bite-sized pieces.

"Quit complaining," she snapped. "If it wasn't for your great uncle Billy's unfortunate snow-blower accident, *I'd* still be sitting with the little kids."

In my family, we also followed the Alaska injunction to share the holidays with others. There was always plenty of food, because my mother thought of any turkey weighing less than twenty-five pounds as scrawny. As a child, I was always happy to see strangers at the table, because they meant fewer leftovers, which in turn meant fewer dinners centered on inventive leftover recipes. I tell you, if I never see another plate of turkey tetrazzini again, it'll be too soon. But my father's habit of inviting anybody and everybody to dinner created some strange dining companions. One Thanksgiving I shared a card table with four people who spoke only what seemed to be Hungarian. Another time, I'm almost sure it was Jimmy Hoffa I saw helping himself to thirds of stuffing when he thought nobody was looking.

You can get through the regular holidays OK, as long as they don't hog the cranberry sauce at the big table. But nothing can prepare you men for the Alaska version of that newest of American holidays, the mid-life crisis.

What? You never thought of the mid-life crisis as a

holiday? Of course it is. It's a holiday from your life. In the rest of the world, all you have to do to celebrate it is join a health club, buy a sports car, or maybe fool around with an aerobics instructor named Brie. Even if you decide to have yourself a full-blown crisis and do all three, that's nothing compared to what's required in Alaska.

For example, did you know

Every Alaska male in a mid-life crisis must climb Mount McKinley?

No? Hey, this is Alaska. The Last Frontier. Where men are men, and they can damn well prove it, even if they are forty-five. That's why there aren't many old men here. But the ones who survive? They look marvelous!

The magic of cruising the bars looking for Mr. Right:
The more you drink, the better he will look.

10 | Alaska Courtship

Or, the Odds Are Good,
but the Goods Are Odd

One way to avoid being alone at the holidays is to start your own family. In Alaska, this may mean getting married.

The first step in the family-starting process is to find an appropriate mate. Meeting the right person can be difficult. In fact, some newcomers are so uneasy about their social prospects that they bring a mate with them, the way other people bring long underwear.

This almost never works. Any arriving couple is likely to consist of a person who loves Alaska and a person who hates the place. The one who hates it survives one winter and says, "Whoa! Cold, dark, and snowy? Been there. Done that. Seen the movie. I'm history." And off they go.

Small wonder that the first rule for newly arrived couples is:

Don't make any long-term plans.

One minute you're headed for a cabin in the wilderness to start a big family, and the next you're arguing about who gets the Motley Crue poster. So, before you buy those cabin plans, make sure both you and your mate can adapt to the rigors of Alaska life. And in case you can't, be sure your personal stuff is clearly marked with your name and Social Security number.

No matter how you enter the mate market, your most difficult task is meeting potential partners. Here are some options:

Cruise the bars. In some parts of the Lower 48, people might look down on you for this. But in Alaska, bars are a focus of social activity. In many places, in fact, they are the *only* focus of social activity. Just remember this: In bars, you are expected to drink. Because alcohol consumption impairs your judgment, this can have disastrous results.

"So it's Friday night, and I'm in the bar looking for romance," a woman of my acquaintance told me. "And there's this guy at the other end of the bar giving me the eye. He might be the world's nicest man — and I don't want you to think I'm so shallow that spiritual values aren't as important to me as physical appearance — but, frankly, he's ugly enough to make a train turn down a dirt road.

"Well, the longer I sit, the more I drink. The more I

drink, the better he looks. Along about closing time, I'm totally in the bag and he looks like Mel Gibson.

"Bingo, another coyote date."

"Coyote date?" I asked.

"Yeah, you know, coyote date," she said. "When you wake up the next morning with your arm under his head, look over, and chew your arm off rather than wake him up."

Ask your friends. They invariably know the perfect someone for you. That's true no matter what condition their personal lives might be in. Take your friend Phyllis, who has had more bad luck with men than Liz Taylor. She's sure to know a fellow who's just perfect.

Usually it turns out he *is* just perfect. For Phyllis, who would really enjoy his detailed explanation of the nesting practices of the grebe. Or his writ-by-writ description of his as-yet unsettled divorce. Or an evening of doing shooters and bowling. You, however, will find this fellow to be less than perfect. A *lot* less.

Try the personal ads. Make sure you have a translator handy. Otherwise, you'll never figure out the meaning of: "Financially independent SWM, 5'8", 170 lb., HWP, black/hazel, n/d, n/s seeks SWF under 24 interested in lifetime partnership. No STD." Is he looking for a date, or investment capital?

Besides, what kind of people advertise in the personals? Desperate people, that's who. So that desperate people will read them and respond. That's you. Desperate enough to consider taking a chance on a classified ad. One that doesn't even include a picture. It's just too depressing.

Order a man by mail. Alaska has a long history of importing mail-order brides. Why not turn the tables? From time to time, a catalog of Alaska men is published, disguised as a magazine about Alaska men. Look, some of these guys have been on "Oprah," so how can you go wrong? At least the catalog has pictures, and, since the men all live in Alaska, you don't have to pay a lot of postage.

Unfortunately, even this approach isn't foolproof. Believe it or not, men have been known to exaggerate their attributes and accomplishments, even in catalogs. Sure, you can sue them for false advertising, but what's the point? Alaskans are always interested in successful litigation, but it's not very romantic.

The fact is, true romance is every bit as elusive in Alaska as it is elsewhere. Women have a better chance of finding it than men, simply because there are more men than women in Alaska. Always have been. The problem is, the place seems to attract men who are a little — how should I put this? — eccentric? This has led Alaska women to adopt a slogan describing their search for Mister Right:

The odds are good, but the goods are odd.

As a result, Alaska women sometimes go overboard. Like the women who compete in the Wilderness Woman Contest in the Road Alaska town of Talkeetna each year. They race down Main Street with a five-gallon bucket of water in each hand, clean a ptarmigan, cut firewood, and serve sandwiches and beer. The winner gets notoriety, if not fame. The losers, and the women spectators, get to bid on bachelors at an auction. Most of the bidders confess they've gone just a touch too long between dates.

Of course, finding a mate is even harder for men, who don't have the odds on their side. But even a blind pig finds an acorn once in a while. So it's possible you'll find your dream mate. Then what?

The first question many Alaskans face about wooing their perfect mate is:

Should I get a divorce first?

Most authorities answer, "Yes." True, there's some risk the new relationship will fall through, leaving you without either loved one or spouse. But the risk of physical injury in some forms of Alaska divorce far outweigh the risk of loneliness.

The next hurdle is:

How do I conceal my true personality?

Face it, if something wasn't seriously wrong with you, you'd already be part of a dynamite relationship. So, the trick is to find out just exactly who your new love is looking for, and be that person. If that perfect someone's mad about origami, and your favorite activity is mud-bogging, this ain't going to be easy. But if love was easy, there wouldn't be a hundred-thousand country-western songs about it.

Once you've answered the main strategic questions, turn your attention to tactics. The first thing you want to do is:

Smother your new love in flattery.

The only thing Alaskans like to hear more than praise of Alaska is praise of themselves. Tell her she's prettier than Susan Butcher's favorite lead dog. Tell him he's studlier than a complete set of snow tires. In Alaska, the rule is:

Flattery cannot be too extravagant.

Be careful, though, not to mix up your compliments. Telling her she's so buff she could hunt bears with a willow switch might be a trifle risky. Telling him his skin is as soft as a moose's nose probably won't have the desired effect. And whatever you do, don't tell him he reminds you of your mother. Even if they do happen to have the same tattoo.

Once you've slathered on the flattery, the next step is:

Impress your new love.

Typically, an Alaskan does this with certain key phrases. "The last time I climbed Denali ..." is a good one. So is, "As I said to the foreman of my gold mine ..." And you can't go far wrong with, "So my father, the billionaire oilman, said to me ..."

But remember that a properly conducted love affair, like a properly conducted feud, has an appropriate pace. Don't rush things.

In most places, that means not letting him get to third base too soon. For Alaskans, it has a special meaning:

Don't take your little snookums snow machining too soon.

Frankly, that first snow machine trip is the peak of

any Alaska relationship. Your snuggle bunny soon discovers that's as thrilling as you get. Let the Arctic Cat out of the bag too soon, and your petite sweetie will be off like a dirty shirt to find someone who really does own a gold mine. So, save screaming through the woods at 80 mph, scaring the dickens out of every living thing in the same time zone, for the right moment.

As the love affair develops, remember this:

You are obliged to tell your friends everything.

Alaska is a big place with a thinly scattered population, and, especially during the winter, Alaskans need all the entertainment they can get. So dish the dirt. It's your social obligation.

Besides, it's an excellent opportunity to renew old acquaintances and make new friends. The minute your friends find out you're serious about someone, they'll tell all their friends. Who will tell all their friends. And so on. Soon, you'll be hearing from people you haven't thought of in years. People you thought had left Alaska. People you thought were dead. You'll also be receiving relationship advice from people you've never met. Who live hundreds of miles away. Whose idea of a lasting relationship is when they wake up in the morning and he's still there.

Feel free to ignore their advice. But don't stop talking. Alaskans love gossip. In fact, the state motto ought to be:

If you can't say something nice about someone, come sit next to me.

You may fall into a mixed relationship: You love the smell of a chain saw, and she's a tree-hugger.

11 | Living Together

*Or, Must Your Relationship
Degenerate into Marriage?*

Moving in with someone new is never easy. In Alaska, where you're trying to cram two people's gear and stuff into one person's double-wide house trailer, it's downright difficult.

You might get lucky and have one of those "mixed" relationships: You're a guy who loves the smell of a chain saw in the morning, and she's a tree-hugger. True, you're going to have many philosophical debates, but at least you won't be trying to shoehorn her four-wheeler into a garage that already holds your four-wheeler, your boat, and pieces of what will be your airplane if you ever get the darn thing put back together. At most, she'll have a canoe, a mountain bike, and packages of freeze-dried veggie stew. Nasty stuff, veggie stew, but it doesn't take up much space.

Think how much worse it would be if she were a pro-development greed head with one of everything you've got, plus a plane that actually flies. Just finding a place to store all her dynamite would be a problem.

You might have to leave your perfectly adequate double-wide and move to some new, bigger place. If only you'd thought about that when you were decorating your trailer, you might not have glued your collection of *Playboy* centerfolds directly to the wood paneling.

The first rule of living together is:

Be prepared to compromise.

Her back-up generator might actually be better than yours. If it's not, so what? She's got a right to keep some of her stuff indoors. Even if she's a greenie, she'll need a place to store all that moral indignation. So buy some beer, invite a few friends over, and knock together that wanigan. You can use the room.

It's not simply a matter of space, either. Some differences will be a matter of taste. You'd be surprised how few women think having an Elle MacPherson calendar in every room constitutes a decorating scheme. Remember, *be flexible.* If she wants to put her Chippendale's calendar up, let her. You might find it harder to be so tolerant if her calendar is one of those save-the-spotted-owl jobs on recycled paper. You might even be tempted to say something like, "I had spotted owl for lunch the other day." Don't. Unless you never want to see her naked again.

Once you are both settled in, you'll find your life has changed completely. Sure, you'll still get up in the morning and go to work. But after work, you'll have to come straight home. Every night. No more of those mid-week fly-bys with your buddies to check out the chicks at the nearest roadhouse. No Friday night trips to the sports bar to catch the Aussie Rules football final. No weekends booming across the tundra with young ladies who really know how to fill a snow machine suit. You're *committed* now.

"Why," you might asked, "can't I just keep living the life I once did?"

Two reasons: First, if you get to run around as you used to, doesn't she? Do you want to straggle in at two a.m. like you did in your bachelor days, then have to wait up an another hour until she gets home? I thought not.

Second, such tear-away behavior violates the most basic rule of any relationship:

You have to sleep sometime.

Try that kind of nonsense and you're likely to wake up duct-taped to the bedpost while she tries to decide which of your golf clubs is just right for knocking some sense into you.

"Let's see," she'll be saying, "do I want loft here? Or distance?"

The fact is, the learning curve in a relationship can be steep, so steep that you could fall off and hurt yourself. But, like snow boarding down the face of a glacier, learning to argue without injury is simple, if you pay attention to the rules:

Know when to argue.

The best time to argue is later, when you are the only one in the room. Then, you can say all the insightful, witty things that you can't say to your mate because you'll get your clock cleaned. When she's around, it's much safer to be agreeable.

Be careful what you say.

People often say things without paying attention to the effect they might have. For instance, you know the phrase, "That's the stupidest thing I ever heard?" Forget that phrase. You're not going to do anything with it but really irritate your mate. Besides, even if you utter that phrase only once, you'll *never* hear the end of it. You'll be sitting together in the Pioneer Home, talking about how much nicer Alaska was before all the riffraff moved in, and she'll ask you if whatever she said forty years ago is still the stupidest thing you've ever heard. So be careful what you say. Good phrases are, "Yes, dear" and "I was wrong."

Be careful how you say it.

Some people can't resist an artful turn of phrase. Take my advice, resist. Samuel Johnson called this kind of phrase-making "talking for victory." Of course, Sam was never married, so how was he to know that saying something like, "You know, dear, when you shriek like that, only dogs can hear you," is a big mistake. You might be thinking to yourself, "What a clever line! Hey, that'll sound great when I repeat it." Only you'll be repeating it to the dog while you're bunking together.

Know when to give up.

Immediately is a good time. It saves a lot of wear and tear on everybody, and you don't have to tiptoe through the argument like it's a minefield. The basic truth about arguing is: The only thing worse than losing an argument with your mate is winning one.

The only thing worse than either of those is forgetting an anniversary. No, not a wedding anniversary. You're not married yet, remember? At least not to this woman. No, it's those other anniversaries, the ones that men always forget.

"You know what the most chilling words in the English language are?" a male friend of mine once asked.

"Every man knows that," I said. "They are: 'Do you know what today is?'"

Have you ever seen that look Wile E. Coyote gets,

when he realizes his latest scheme to catch Beep Beep the Roadrunner has just failed, in a way that's about to become very painful? That's the look a man gets when his significant other asks if he knows what today is, and he doesn't know. Of course, he doesn't know. Men don't keep track. You could tell a guy it's the fourth anniversary of the first time he did the laundry, and he wouldn't know any different. Guys, never, ever forget an anniversary. And since you know perfectly well that you're going to forget — you're a guy, remember? — always keep a small store of gifts close at hand.

"What?" you can exclaim. "It's the second anniversary of the first time we saw a moose together? This must be for you."

Then you give her a diamond bracelet.

As long as you follow the rules, your relationship can survive indefinitely. But sooner or later, you will come to that critical point. The zip is gone, the passion spent. She doesn't even complain when you decide to rebuild your snow machine engine in the kitchen.

When that happens, etiquette dictates that you do one of two things:

You can go out for a pack of cigarettes and never come back.

This will allow the abandoned former object of your desire to laugh, to weep, to put a price on your head. It also gives her the pick of the belongings. This is the gentlemanly thing to do.

A surprising number of people lack the moral fiber to do the right thing. Instead, they chose Option Two:

Try to save a failing relationship by getting married.

Even people who have been married before do that. Samuel Johnson — remember him? — called this "the triumph of hope over experience." If so, Alaska has to be one of the most hopeful places on earth, judging from the number of grooms who make it to the altar despite staggering child-support payments.

If, that is, an altar is used. There are a great number of church weddings, it's true, primarily because there are a great number of churches. Big churches and little churches, rural churches and urban churches, not to mention one of every kind of Baptist church there is. In fact, there are nearly as many churches in Alaska as there are bars. Nearly, but not quite. In Alaska, the devil is running just ahead of Jesus, but the race is close.

Anyway, church weddings in Alaska are about the same as church weddings anywhere. You send out invitations, people send gifts. There's a wedding, then a reception. The guests throw rice, the bride throws a bouquet. The bride's father looks at the bill and throws a fit.

Through it all, you listen to all the usual advice. Your friends advise you not to tie yourself down, that you can do better. Her friends advise her to reject your proposal:

"Why buy the cow when you're getting the milk for free?" they ask her.

Yet, you both ignore this advice and get to the church on time.

Assuming a church is involved.

In Alaska, you can get married anywhere.

The vows are just as likely to be said in the bride's favorite clearing in the woods, or at the groom's favorite jet-ski dealership. People get married on top of mountains, next to their favorite fishing hole, or during the start of the Iditarod Trail Sled Dog Race. These affairs have a typically Alaska flavor that church weddings often lack, particularly during the reception. As those who attended these recent nuptials discovered.

A thirty-something woman named Deborah married a fellow named Flatbed in the Road Alaska town of Kenny Lake. According to the reports of the Alaska State Troopers, the reception featured wine, marijuana, and gunfire.

The next day, as the reception continued, a neighbor named John dropped by, drawn by curiosity about the celebratory gunfire of the day before. Deborah persuaded John, just for fun, to try getting out of a pair of handcuffs she and Flatbed had received as a wedding present. John said sure, put the cuffs on, and couldn't escape.

At the trial, the stories told by Deborah and John diverged. The version the jury believed is that Deborah decided to show John what a good shot she was by shooting the handcuffs off. She pulled out a .22 and shot him in the hand.

All in all, it was a perfect example of a Road Alaska wedding, topped only by the defense attorney's description of the subsistence lifestyle of Kenny Lake: "They fish, they hunt, they drink, they farm."

If you're rushing to the hospital in a dog sled, just let the dogs worry about how to get there.

12 | Time to Have Kids

*Or, What to Do When
Your Biological Clock Goes Off*

As soon as you finish taking your wedding vows, your parents begin asking: "When are we going to be grandparents?"

They want to become grandparents because they know perfectly well that it's a job with no responsibilities. They can show up at your place, spoil the kid rotten, then leave. No diaper changing for them, or walking the floor all night with a colicky baby. Nope, they already did that with you. Now they want you to have the same experience. In short, they want revenge.

The polite thing to do is make excuses.

"I'm sorry, mom," you can say, "but Herb's actually an alien from the Crab Nebula. Cross-breeding is out of the question."

Forget it. Even if your mother is willing to believe your spouse is an alien — "I knew it," she'll say, "no human being could be *that* lazy" — your parents are not going to be happy until you are suffering just like they did. Plus, they know they'll get to give you advice.

"Teething, is she?" they'll say. "The perfect cure for that is a big slug of whiskey. No, you don't give it to the baby. You take it internally. It'll dull the pain of listening to the baby cry. Which she's going to do non-stop for the next eighteen months. Yuk, yuk, yuk."

Even though many etiquette experts frown on the practice, you can tell them to mind their own business. Politely. Say something like, "I really think this is something Herb and I have to decide for ourselves."

Good luck. You know what your mom is going to say: "I carried you in my body for nine months for this? So you can talk to me like that with your fresh mouth?"

If, like a lot of other parents of Alaskans, they live somewhere far, far away, consider this solution:

Move, leave no forwarding address, change your telephone number.

Not that it will do you any good. You might get a

couple of weeks of peace and quiet, but what sort of mood do you think your mother is going to be in when she finds you again?

"You must have forgotten to have your new number listed, dear," she'll say sweetly. "But once I cornered the president of AT&T in the locker room of his golf club, getting the new listing was surprisingly easy."

Then, she'll give your number to your sisters, brothers. aunts, uncles, cousins, nieces, and nephews, and all of them will call to ask when you're going to have kids.

Unfortunately, at least one of you might turn out to be in league with your parents. Women apparently have something called a biological clock, which goes off when you are running out of time to reproduce. No matter how often you hit the snooze button, you still hear the clock saying, "It's getting late. You're thirty-seven. Time to have kids."

In Alaska, not everyone waits until their middle years to reproduce. Or, until they are married, for that matter. A common first sign of pregnancy is when a young man snow-machines over to visit his girlfriend and finds himself looking down the barrel of her dad's shotgun. But many people wait until their acne clears up before having children of their own. And those who aren't married usually stampede to the altar at the first sign of pregnancy. That sign is usually you, wrapped around the commode in the morning.

In announcing the pregnancy, you and your spouse should follow proper etiquette. For him, that means using good phrasing like, "We're expecting a blessed event." Not bad phrasing like, "Hey, I knocked up the old lady."

Good: "We're having a baby."

Bad: "She's got a bun in the oven."

Good: "My wife is pregnant."

Bad: "The rabbit died."

If he doesn't seem to get it, remind him that, as far as nature is concerned, his job is finished and he's pretty much superfluous now.

Once you've got the announcements out of the way, you have to begin preparing for the baby's arrival.

First, sell a bunch of his gear.

If he complains, remind him he's going to be a father, and if he thinks that means he's going to go off into the woods with his good-for-nothing friends while you stay home and raise the baby, he's got another think coming.

Next, turn the wanigan into a nursery.

Once all the old airplane parts are gone, there will be plenty of room for a crib and a rocker. Your mate will have a wonderful time wrestling with the ducky-and-bunny wallpaper, and putting up the frilly curtains.

Finally, go to childbirth classes.

One of the things your mother forgot to mention was how much easier childbirth was in her day. Your father hung out in the waiting room, smoking cigarettes, while they wheeled your mom into the delivery room and gave her enough pain killers to drop a musk ox in its tracks. Then they simply removed you by using what Bill Cosby calls "the salad spoons." Which accounts for those pictures where your head is shaped like a yam.

You and your spouse should be so lucky. These days, the two of you are expected to approach pregnancy as a team, although you know perfectly well who gets the morning sickness, water retention, and lower back pain. Some team. And you are expected to take classes from cheerful women who will assure you that breathing techniques can take the place of drugs during childbirth. Yeah, right.

In short, they're telling you that despite hundreds of years of medical advances, you're supposed to have this baby just like the cavewomen did. Except that you'll be surrounded by hundreds of thousands of dollars worth of medical equipment nobody is using, while your own personal hunter-gatherer tells you how to breathe.

Well, at least you can divert yourself from this grim prospect by choosing a name for the baby. Alaska names often follow national trends, which is why there are so many ten-year-old girls named Brie.

And your family is sure to have a nickel's worth of advice, like if it's a girl, naming her after your aunt Sophronia.

But there are plenty of skookum Alaska monikers to slap on the kid, names that call to mind the grandeur of life in the north. For example, if it's a boy, you can call him Yukon. If it's a girl, you can call her Susitna. And if they're twins, you can call them Smith & Wesson.

But you can spend only so much time listening to your mother's advice, going to classes, and trying to figure out who the heck would name a kid Herkimer. Sooner or later, you will have to have the baby. This is an occasion fraught with social obligations.

Labor pains must begin in the middle of the night.

This will enable you to wake your spouse by grabbing him by whatever body part is nearest when the first pain hits. Then, after you manage to gasp out your news and he manages to extricate himself from your grip, he can run around in circles, cawing, and flapping his arms.

If you give birth in winter, whatever vehicle you'd planned on taking to the hospital won't start. Remain calm. When your spouse races in with the bad news, simply pick up your bag, grab him by the ear, and walk him slowly out the door. Then point out that he'd have a lot better luck hitching the dogs so their noses point *away* from the sled. Or, as the case may be, that he's not going to get far trying to start the car with the house key.

Don't be a backseat driver.

In fact, for the safety of you, your baby, your spouse, and everyone else on the road at that hour, you'd do better driving yourself.

If your spouse insists on driving, simply keep your eyes closed, except when the vehicle tilts to an angle of more than a forty-five-degrees. Of course, if you're making the trip by dog sled, just do what all the veteran mushers do: Leave the whole business to the dogs.

More and more women are having babies at home, which may seem like an attractive idea. But think of all the fun they miss getting to the hospital.

Once you get to the hospital, it's time to do what you learned in class. Relax. Breathe. Listen to your coach. This state of mind will last for a couple of hours, until you just can't stand the sound of his voice anymore. Then, just send him away on some errands.

"Darling," you'll say sweetly, "would you mind running to Seattle for a double skinny latte."

Remember every detail
of this blessed event.

Your family and friends will want to enjoy it, too. And there's nothing like being able to recall the exact number of times your spouse fell asleep during your labor, or how, when you sent him for ice chips, he got to chatting with a couple of attractive candy stripers and didn't return for ninety minutes.

Somewhere in here, serious labor will begin. Stay in control. Easy for me to say. I have no first-hand knowledge of what labor is like, but I do remember Carol Burnett's advice: "You men want to experience something like labor? Take your lower lip and stretch it over your head."

If you don't stay in control, ugly things could happen. When that first big pain hits, you might treat the entire labor room to a colorful account of your spouse's ancestry. Or, a lively description of what you're going to do to him when you heal. He is responsible for your condition, of course. And while you are suffering like the damned, he's giving you advice while waving a video cam in your face.

"Breathe, huh?" you might say. "Lean in close here, and I'll show you how to breathe out of another part of your body."

You might also re-evaluate your commitment to natural childbirth.

"I don't care how peasant women do it," you might scream. "I want drugs. Lots of drugs. NOW!"

This is the sort of behavior that might be unnerving to the other mothers-to-be. Not to mention patients throughout the hospital, and anybody within a five-block radius. So if you absolutely have to tell your spouse what to do with that video cam, do it in a venomous whisper.

Eventually they'll wheel you into the delivery

room, where your doctor — most likely a man who doesn't know a damn thing about real pain — will make bad jokes and try to talk you out of a full anesthetic. Listen to him. If he knocks you out, you'll miss seeing your spouse pass out at the first sign of blood. The wimp.

No matter how unlikely it seems at the time, your labor will come to an end and you will be a mother. Almost immediately, your body will begin to manufacture a chemical that will make you forget the whole experience. If it didn't, no one would ever have a second child.

No matter how wonderful you feel as your spouse wheels you and your baby out of the hospital for the trip home, don't be smug. Believe it or not, the hard part of being a parent has just begun.

When you take the baby outdoors in winter, you'll bundle her like a mummy. This is perfectly natural.

13 | Bringing Up Baby

*Or, Tips for Saving Your
Slim Whitman Records*

As soon as you bring your infant home from the hospital, you'll face the first obstacle in rearing an Alaska child: The new grandmothers will want to visit. Even though the grandmothers will have to stay with you,

Invite both grandmothers, anyway.

This is not a question of manners; it is a question of survival. Nothing in human experience — not war, not pestilence, famine, or television sitcoms — is worse than the wrath of a new granny invited to be the *second* visitor. You'd have a better chance of keeping all your body parts in working order if you went naked bodysurfing on a glacier.

The grandmothers will claim they just want to help the new mother. But you know perfectly well that they are coming north to begin their insidious child-spoiling campaign. Not to mention sowing seeds of discontent by saying things like: "Isn't this trailer a little small for the three of you?" To keep them under control, do what Alaskans have done with visiting relatives since the Klondike Gold Rush:

Put them to work.

In some quarters, I'm told, putting house guests to work is considered bad manners. No doubt those quarters are constantly littered with house guests. Alaskans have learned the value of making guests work. They feel wanted. They get things get done. And they leave promptly. They have to. They're exhausted.

This approach to hosting is so well accepted that it's common for neighbors to ask to borrow your guests.

"Hey," they say, "my pipes are clogged again and I need new wood paneling in the rec room. Can I borrow your father-in-law for a week?"

"Sure," you'll reply, "as long as you'll lend me your mom the next time she visits. The drive train on my Weasel needs work."

So don't feel bad. Put those new grandmothers to work. Start right off by making them responsible for the birth announcements.

In the past, birth announcements were simple. The

new father burst out the front door and emptied his revolver into the air. The neighbors heard the gunshots and knew the baby had been born. But:

Gunshots are appropriate to any occasion.

They can announce a marriage. Or finalize a divorce. Or tell the neighbors that the authorities are trying to collect back child support again. As the population grew, and people were unable to keep up with their neighbors' lives, the meaning of gunshots became ambiguous.

"Now, what do those gunshots mean?" people found themselves asking one another. "Did the Smiths have their baby? Or did Mrs. Jones find out about her husband and the barmaid?"

As a result, even Alaskans now send written announcements. Little cards with a baby and some birds in soft pastels on the front, with "Damn! Another mouth to feed!" written on the inside are popular.

When that chore is finished, you can set the grandmothers to other tasks such as pureeing caribou haunch for baby food, sewing baby's first blanket from muskrat furs, and fashioning tiny-tot wind gear from duct tape. The trick is to keep them busy. That way, they won't be able to pick the baby up every time she cries, talk baby talk to her, and otherwise program her to expect to be the center of the universe.

Once the grandmothers leave — hopefully, not before they fix that balky generator — you'll be on your own. Soon, you'll understand what Gallagher, the comedian, meant when he said: "We have a baby at our house." Pause. "All day long." What you'll learn is this:

Your household has gone from being you-centered to being baby-centered.

You'll learn that in the middle of the day, when you fall asleep at your desk because you were up all night walking the floor with a fretful child. You'll learn it in the middle of the night, when you're on the way to the bathroom and you step on the baby's wooden ducky pull toy. And you'll learn it unforgettably if either the ducky's quacking or your cries of pain wake the baby, causing your wife to fly out of bed in exactly the frame of mind seen only in sleep-deprived new mothers and wounded grizzly bears.

"Splint your own damn leg," she'll snarl. "I've got to feed the baby."

The situation will not improve as the baby gets older. Soon, she'll be able to get around on her own, a development that will get your attention the day she destroys your Slim Whitman albums.

That's the signal to baby-proof your house. Put all your guns and ammo out of reach. Move the snow machine engine out of the kitchen. Pack away your collection of painted gold pans. That will solve some problems, but not others. The dog will still have a nervous breakdown from being tugged, pulled, and poked. Then, the gag gifts from the grandparents will begin arriving: drum sets, child-sized electric guitars with full-volume Fender Stratocaster amps, battery-powered chain saws. Anything that makes noise, your child will soon have two of.

Then, there are the terrors of physical development. Every time she tries to walk, you'll rush around with arms outstretched to catch her, like a punt returner who knows perfectly well he should have called for a fair catch. You'll run into a door frame yourself because you were watching her topple into the stereo equipment instead of paying attention to where you were going as you rushed to catch her.

About the same time, she'll start teething. This apparently minor development will cause wholesale changes in your life. You can kiss sleeping goodbye for the next six months; babies cut teeth at all hours, and never quietly. Everything below knee level will be soaked in drool. She'll chew on anything, including your nose, and those little buggers can bite.

The list of firsts grows: First time that, while trying to pull herself up, she pulls the tablecloth — and everything on it — onto the floor. First visit to the emergency room (these are sometimes the same event). First word spoken — all too often something she heard you say after you ran into the door jamb, which she utters when your minister has dropped by to see how things are going. Life with a toddler is never uneventful.

But the real Alaska challenge is dressing your child for the outdoors. The rule followed by Alaska mothers since time immemorial is:

If any skin shows,
add another layer.

This means that when you take the baby out, she will be so well bundled up that she will have to breathe through a snorkel. Your friends will ask: "Is this the new baby, or are you taking your clothes to the cleaners?" If, however, the infant is not properly bundled, perfect strangers will start selling raffle tickets to raise money for more clothes.

The rules don't change once the baby becomes a toddler. If a child is going outdoors during the winter, let this be the rule:

There is no such thing
as too many clothes.

When I was a child, my friends and I looked like laundry hampers with feet. Our mothers put so many clothes on us we could hardly move. That not only kept us from getting frostbite, it kept us from getting into mischief, too. We knew perfectly well that we couldn't run away; glaciers could move faster than we could.

If, by some miracle, our own mothers didn't bundle us up so that we looked like tiny versions of Boris Karloff in "The Mummy," somebody else's mother would.

"Hold still," they'd say. "I'm sure I've got another Air Force survival parka in your size somewhere."

At some point during your child's toddling years, you'll have to decide whether to have another child.

Your wife, completely befuddled by those memory-wiping postpartum chemicals, will be game. Besides, if you have two, they might keep one another busy. And you want to be a parent, don't you? You know what Bill Cosby said about parenthood. He said, "I don't consider people with only one child to be parents, because when something goes wrong, they already know who did it."

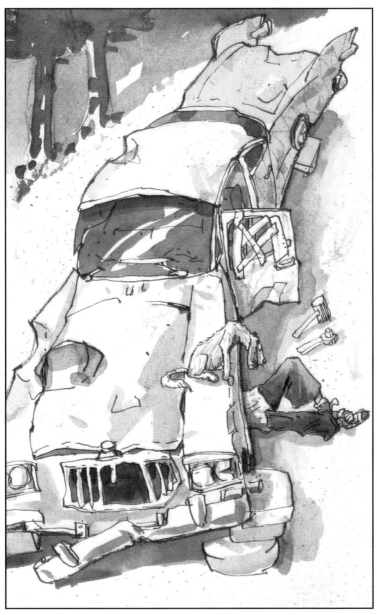

Alaska is full of junked cars littering the landscape, so you might as well buy your teenager one.

14 | The Mother's Curse

*Or, Yipes, They've
Become Teenagers!*

One nice thing about having a second child is that the grandmothers won't be falling all over themselves to visit. Second children, as any second child knows, have to battle for every shred of attention they get.

"Another child?" the grandmothers will say. "How nice. Can't visit at the moment. Must defend the mah-jongg title I won on last year's Caribbean cruise. But I'll send a check."

If you have a third child, all they'll send is a pamphlet from Zero Population Growth.

By this time, you'll be so deep into parenthood you think you'll never get out. You will realize that the Mother's Curse has worked. You remember the Mother's Curse: "When you grow up, I hope you have children just like you."

It might be something as simple as a tantrum during the terrible twos, that period between eighteen months and eighteen years when your child becomes as difficult as Chinese arithmetic. Or, it may be when you overhear your child telling her friends that she really isn't a member of your family, but a princess sent to live with you by mistake.

"These people are so common," she'll say. "Surely you can see that I couldn't possibly be the daughter of a woman with skin like that."

Or, it could be the first time the neighbor brings home your child, a baseball, and a bill for a broken picture window.

Incidents like these, of which there were more than a few in my childhood, raise the question of how to deal with other people's children. In Alaska, the rules are simple:

Treat them like your own.

If they are around your house at dinner time, feed them. If they are there when you leave for the movies, take them. And, if they do something they shouldn't, punish them.

I'll never forget the first time somebody else's mom caught us engaged in some childish prank — I think we were trying to set fire to a cat — and spanked the lot of us. I ran home, crying.

"Mrs. Smith spanked me with a switch!" I cried.

"Oh, she did, did she?" my mother said. "We'll soon see about that."

She called the other mother on the telephone.

"Zelda," she said. "This is Mike's mom. He says you spanked him with a switch. Well, I'm calling to tell you that the next time you feel it's necessary to spank my child — let me know. I've got a perfectly good belt hanging right here."

This was, of course, when Alaska's child-abuse law was still "spare the rod, spoil the child." That was before each child was assigned a lawyer upon leaving the hospital nursery.

Although the rules have changed, it is still possible to teach a child manners – provided the child's lawyer agrees that no legal rights are being infringed and the child's psychologist is of the opinion that the process will not hamper self-actualization.

Here are the manners every proper Alaska child should know:

Alaska children should be neither seen nor heard. This is particularly true on fine summer evenings, when your child finds himself in a neighbor's garden, harvesting carrots. It would be thoughtless to disturb the neighbor. He needs his rest, after having done all the hoeing, planting, weeding, and watering. If a bad-mannered child were to disturb him, he might object. And the objection might take the form of bird shot, which leads us to the second rule.

If they are seen or heard, Alaska children should

keep low to the ground. None of this disruptive scream-ing and running. What will the neighbors think? Instead, children should crawl as fast as they can to the shelter of the kohlrabi, wriggle back under the fence, then hot-foot it out of there. That way, they will avoid such embarrassing possibilities as running full tilt into a tree and knocking themselves out, or causing the neighbor to curse so loudly he loses his voice. A properly brought up child will remember to take the bag off the head of the neighbor's mean dog on his way out.

Alaska children respect their parents. If, for in-stance, a child should happen to be up late at night getting a drink of water and spot her father crawling in the door, she should not wake up her mother to come look. Instead, she should keep quiet, accept his excuse that he sprained his ankle playing basketball, and help him navigate. If he should suddenly burst into song, she should not join in. Instead, she should run like the wind before her mother appears.

Alaska children should not speak unless spoken to. It's not polite to just blurt out the names of co-con-spirators. If, for example, a policeman should happen to catch a kid with more comic books than a kid could afford, the kid should not tell him right out who di-verted the storekeeper's attention and who held the bikes. He should attempt to plea bargain first.

Alaska children should not talk back. If his mother tells him to do the dishes, he shouldn't give her a bunch of lip. He should use the chore as a growth opportu-nity, in this case a chance to develop his motor skills by doing the dishes and practicing his juggling at the same time. If he happens to drop something, what the heck. They aren't his dishes.

Alaska children should turn the other cheek when mooning cop cars.

Alaska children should know that it's better to give than to receive. If it's punches, flu germs, or insults we're talking about. Otherwise, a child should grab as much as she can and worry about what it is later.

In sum:

Teach Alaska children to act like Alaska adults.

It's the only way they'll survive.

If they follow these rules, and don't mouth off to the bigger kids, your children ought to survive to become teenagers. Talk about your mixed blessing. Teenagers can get into more mischief in a week than they have in the entire rest of their lives. For proof, stop right here and think for a moment about your own teen years. Scary, isn't it?

Unfortunately, to get from childhood to adulthood, every human being must pass through the non-human period known as teenage. (As a matter of policy, parents should not use the words "teen" and "hood" together, for fear that when their child becomes one, he or she will become the other, too.)

At no time in a child's development does the Mother's Curse cause a parent more difficulty. A father remembers racing around an icy Deadman's

Curve at seventy mph in his mother's car, which was full of other teens and open beer bottles, then tries to imagine his son doing the same thing. All he can see is flashing lights and a rescue crew using the jaws of life. A mother remembers going out with the fastest boy in her high school, wearing a skirt so short the material wouldn't have made a decent pocket handkerchief. Then, she thinks about what her own daughter might do in a situation like that, and suddenly Mom is prematurely gray.

Alaska parents have developed several methods of dealing with the trauma of teenage, methods that work for them if not the teenagers. They are:

Send them away. Favorite destinations are military school for boys and a convent for girls. Out of sight doesn't merely mean out of mind, it often means out of jail, too. A big advantage here is Alaska's isolation, which means that the kid won't be able to hitchhike home easily. Sure, it's expensive, but so are lawyers, bail, and those outfits girls like to wear these days to look like Madonna.

Send them away. Fortunately for Alaska parents, the state is so big that they can send their teens far away and the kids will still meet the Alaska Permanent Fund residency requirement. A favorite trick of urban parents is to send their kid to stay with family in Rural Alaska. A couple of months in the Bush can only have good results. The kid might hate it, in which case he or she will shape up just to be allowed to stay in town. Believe me, a summer in Bethel would have turned Soapy Smith into a priest. Or the kid might love it, in which case he or she will want to stay far enough away that the parents won't know exactly what's going on.

Lock them in a closet and shove food under the door until they turn eighteen. This is an approach particularly favored by fathers of teenaged daughters. A mother might be afraid her daughter will act like she did, but a father is absolutely certain that every teenaged boy will act like he did.

Maintain plausible deniability. Hey, if it works for presidents, why not for parents? The truth is, all the parents of teenagers want is for them to survive the experience without doing something that will screw up their entire lives. Otherwise, frankly, the parents just don't want to know. So, they don't go looking for trouble. They are especially careful to stay out of the kid's room, which they'd need biohazard suits to enter, anyway.

Buy them their own cars. In most places, this might be a bad move. But Alaska is full of old junkers, and buying a teen one of them has many advantages. First, the teen will have to spend so much time and energy keeping the car running that he or she will have little left for finding trouble. Second, the car will soak up the money the young man might have spent at the pool hall or the young woman might have spent on a Madonna outfit. Third, old cars are massive and slow-moving, so that when the kid smacks a moose or ends up flipped over in a ditch

along an icy highway, he or she won't have been going fast enough to get hurt badly. Fourth, the
thoughtless little creep won't be borrowing your car
all the time and bringing it home with an empty gas
tank.

Whatever you decide to do, remember:

Your goal is not to make
the teen years enjoyable.

Your goal is to make the teen years *survivable*, for
the teen and for you. And if you are successful, the
child will thank you for your trouble by leaving home.

In Alaska, that usually means going far, far away.
Alaska is a wonderful place, but for anyone who
grows up here, the important road is the one leading
out. Some kids join the military, some go to college,
some just decide to wander the earth, like Caine in
"Kung Fu." When your child tells you he or she is
leaving, just remember: Keep a straight face. Do not
dance around the room, pumping your fist and shouting "Yes! Yes! YES!" You'll hurt the child's feelings.
Instead, wait until the last child sets out, then sell the
house — it'll be too big for the two of you, anyway
— and move without leaving a forwarding address.
Most kids will take the hint.

You'll have to move quickly. In recent years,
there's been a frightening development for parents,
a child called a boomeranger. That's a kid who goes
out into the world, doesn't like it, and moves back in
with you before you can sell the house. Some of these

children come back more than once. This development is a wonderful argument for having closely spaced children, and, as they get older, keeping a real-estate agent on standby.

Your goal is to raise healthy, happy children who become contributing members of society, children who will grow into adults you love and respect. At a distance.

The wife gets the assets, the husband gets the debts, and you both get to spend time with lawyers.

15 | Divorce and Remarriage

Or, Adding Insult to Injury

Alaskans value the institution of marriage. Many of them value it so much they marry over and over again. As a result, many Alaskans who call themselves bachelors are in fact former husbands. One reason "the goods are odd" is that they consist in large part of other women's castoffs.

"Alaska is full of used men," says a woman I know. "Unfortunately, most of them are all used up."

Like everything else in Alaska, you can get a debate on this point. Some Alaska women value once-married men. They see that first marriage as a sort of finishing school, where some other woman has sanded off the man's rougher edges. Under this theory, a once-married man is older, wiser, and a lot less cocky. A woman friend insists that the first rule of survival for women in Alaska is:

Never be somebody's first wife.

This rule would apply to men, too, if men weren't completely uninterested in marriage, divorce, and any of the other legal technicalities. Men are only interested in chasing women, catching women, and then making their escape. There's a word for men who fail to make a clean getaway: husbands.

Men get married not because they want to, but because it's the easiest thing to do. They get divorced for the same reason. Women know this. They might pretend that the man is the boss, but deep down inside they possess a secret passed from one generation of women to the next but rarely, if ever, spoken aloud: Men are simple. All they want is some simple form of entertainment — fishing, say, or watching football — a steady supply of beer, and affection. Keeping a man isn't that much different from keeping a dog, although dogs rarely make good fly fishermen and actually prefer water to beer.

Male simplicity has its downside, too. All men, whether married or not, live by one simple rule the world over. That rule is expressed in different ways in different languages. In Alaska, it is most commonly expressed as:

It ain't cheatin' if you don't get caught.

That means that a man will say almost anything to

a pretty woman. He can't help it. If he's been married forty years and has twelve kids, the poor schnook won't just tell her he's single. He'll tell her he's independently wealthy, too.

This behavior is usually harmless. My women friends say they can always tell when a man is lying.

"If his lips are moving, he's lying," they say.

Every once in a while, a man and a woman will have a simultaneous lapse in judgment. He'll start believing whatever nonsense he's telling her, and she'll believe it, too. Unfortunately, if his wife doesn't believe whatever nonsense he's telling *her*, the result is sometimes worse than divorce. It's a Spenard Divorce.

The Spenard Divorce is named after a section of Anchorage that contains a lot of bars. The typical Spenard Divorce works like this:

A man and a woman are sitting together, usually *very* close together, in a crowded bar. Another woman walks in, spots them, and walks over. Once she gets near their table, she pulls a gun from her purse.

"You two-timing weasel," she yells.

"But baby, you don't understand," the man cries. "She's my personal trainer. We're discussing diet."

"Diet, huh?" the woman screams. "I've got your diet right here. Eat hot lead!"

Then, she starts shooting. People, glasses, and chairs scatter in every direction.

By the time she is out of ammo, several people — husband, girlfriend, innocent bystanders — could have holes in them. If the husband dies as a result, the wife is said to have gotten a Spenard Divorce. If he survives, they usually end up in a boring old courtroom.

Thus, once you've decided your spouse is cheating and you want a divorce, the most important question to ask is:

If I have the right weapon, is a lawyer really necessary?

A lawyer will be necessary if there's property to divide. That's why you're better off making sure your stuff is all clearly marked. Especially if you are a man. In Alaska, divorce settlements are based on the traditional property division:

The wife gets the assets, the husband gets the debts.

Another drawback is that you have to spend time with lawyers. Alaskans may rank them a cut above federal employees, but that's still a cut below lepers.

Once the property has been divided, you are on your own. The tradition in Alaska is for a person who is newly divorced to get drunk, fire shots in the air, and offer to fight all comers, including policemen. Men are expected to act really crazy. But, after you sober up and make bail, you find that you are back at square one. This isn't so bad for the woman, who now has a snow machine for every day of the week and knows what to look for in a man. Basically, an Alaska woman is looking for a man who is a good provider, doesn't drink or smoke, and enjoys attending cultural events. That's why she's still looking.

An Alaska man is looking for something much simpler:

He is looking for a babe.

His biggest problem is what to do if the difference in their ages is bigger than her IQ. If her chest measurement is bigger than his bank account. If what seems to him to be the recent past seems to her to be ancient history. In other words, he has the same problems as any American male with a woman younger than the wine he drinks.

Still, these problems do not prevent people from remarrying. An Alaska woman might not find her ideal, but she might stumble across a guy who isn't allergic to work, is sober once in a while, and likes country music. And an Alaska man might find a babe. If they do, don't quote the line about remarriage being the triumph of hope over experience.

They'll hate you when it turns out you're right.

An elderly ammo-maker is a rare sight, particularly one who isn't singed from his latest explosion.

16 | Aging in Alaska

Or, Don't Grow Old Gracefully

Aging is the price you pay for survival. As a friend of mine told me when I was complaining about the aches and pains of middle age: "Consider the alternative."

Alaskans don't like to admit they're getting old. Blame their peculiar combination of immaturity and active lifestyles. If, for instance, you say an Alaskan is too old to climb Denali carrying a wood stove, watch out. After she's done it, she's likely to tell you you're too old to swim the Yukon carrying a wood stove. And you can't just let a challenge like that pass.

So, the first rule here is:

Never tell an Alaskan he or she is getting old.

If nothing else, whoever you tell is sure to respond, "Yeah? Well, I figure I'm still young enough to whip you." And then try to prove it.

Besides, Alaskans are like everybody else. They *know* when they're getting old. In Alaska, you know you're getting old when:

You can't party all night and work all day. I'll never forget the first time I walked out of a bar at five a.m. on a summer's morning and couldn't see a thing. "Jeez, I've gone blind," I thought, "I guess I'm too old for this." Fortunately, all that was wrong was I'd forgotten my sun glasses. But it made me stop and think, I'll tell you. What I thought was, "I wish I could have one more cold beer before I get to the office."

Other people aren't so lucky.

"You know," a friend told me recently. "I think I'm slowing down."

"Why do you think that?" I asked.

"Well," he said, dropping his voice. "Lately, after I've been out five or six nights in a row, I actually have to go home and catch a couple of hours of sleep."

You start buying commercial ammo. No Alaskan worth the name uses commercial loads. You never can tell when one of those mass-produced cartridges will misfire. A bear might be charging. You might have a shot at a brand new road sign.

Besides, you need some punch behind your slugs. If you're ever in a position where you have to fire through a moose to hit a bear, you're never going to do it with puny, under-powered commercial shells.

So Alaskans make their own, pouring special mixtures of powder into shell casings, inserting their own special alloy slugs, crimping the whole thing together, and going on to the next. That way, they get ammo they can trust, not to mention a rush from the risk of blowing themselves to kingdom come by dropping a cigarette into the gunpowder. And if an airplane flies over and enraged elephants parachute out, they'll have just the right load for the job.

As you might imagine, making ammo requires a steady hand and keen eyesight. So, an old ammo-maker is a rare sight, particularly an old ammo-maker without scars from his most-recent explosion.

You lose track of the stories you've told. This symptom is one of the worst. Alaskans are expected to tell stories, and not allow an excessive regard for the truth to get in the way. Over the years, most Alaskans embellish their tales until they become — lies is such a harsh word — creative nonfiction. These stories age like fine wine. Unfortunately, so do their tellers. And some of the details start to blur. Soon, the people you're telling the story to know it better than you do.

"Wait a second," they say. "I thought the bear was 1200 pounds and the salmon was 120."

People stop listening to your stories altogether. An Alaskan without stories is like a Hawaiian without an aloha shirt. A sad, sad sight.

"Too bad," they say. "That guy was once a great storyteller. Now he's so forgetful, he could hide his own Easter eggs."

You start telling your friends to act their age. I saw a particularly ugly example of this not too long ago, two guys arguing over lunch at a roadhouse.

"You're acting like a damn fool," one said. "It's about time you started acting your age."

"Me acting my age, huh?" the other said. "Who was it arm-wrestling with those truck drivers? Winning the Frug-dancing contest? Setting a new roadhouse record for tequila shooters? That wasn't me. That was you."

"True," the first one said. "But it wasn't me hot-wired that bulldozer and drove it into the river. Or stole the State Trooper's hat and wouldn't give it back. That was you."

"You're right," the second one said. "But so what? I ain't old. I'm barely a day over seventy. You've got to be, what? Seventy-two? Seventy-three??"

"What difference does that make?" the first guy said. "You have to grow old, but you don't have to grow up."

You put on an Alaska tuxedo. This is the surest sign of aging in Alaska. You see somebody in a Filson suit, a drip-dry shirt and a bolo tie, and you're looking at an Alaskan who is telling the world that he's getting old. Just don't call him "old-timer," unless you're looking for a painful lesson in manners.

Fortunately, growing old has an upside. Once you reach a ripe old age, the state will give you money every month. Even better, you will outlive your contemporaries. This might seem like bad manners in some quarters. But somebody's got to do it. Besides, in

Alaska, living life to the fullest is the best possible behavior.

After all, there are few pleasures greater — at your age, anyway — than going to the funeral of someone you couldn't stand. You can limp on in, look down at the deceased in his coffin, and loudly say: "Somebody get me a straight pin. I want to make sure this SOB ain't faking." Everyone will chuckle indulgently, and people will trip all over themselves to help you to your seat.

Even if you can't make it to the funeral, reading the obituaries can be a source of satisfaction.

"Well, I'll be," you can tell your cronies, "it says here old Creeper Johnson died. I'd have thought some jealous husband would'a killed him years ago."

Saying things like this will give you a reputation as a plain-spoken, salt-of-the-earth type.

Growing old means you can say whatever the Hell you want.

Think some woman's hat looks dopey? Say so. She'll just giggle and say, "Oh, isn't that cute?" Unless she's your age, in which case she's likely to punch your lights out.

Not only will you get to tell the truth, but you also will be able to expand your repertoire of lies. If you live long enough,

You can take credit for anything that happened during your life.

"Sure, the history books say Hudson Stuck was the

first to climb Denali," you can say. "But I was really first. That Stuck just hogged all the credit. You'd have thought a bishop would be more honest."

And if the people you're talking to are Cheechakos, you can get away with almost anything.

"Yup, I built the Alaska Highway single-handed," you can tell them. "Couldn't wait for the Army. All that paperwork, they wouldn't have had the damn thing finished by the Gulf War."

Old people everywhere get away with this sort of nonsense. But in Alaska they're not just tolerated for it. They're worshipped.

They aren't just mouthy old geezers,
they're elders.

What they say is respected.

What a racket. You know what the elders say, don't you? They say two things. They say the old days were better. And they say you'd better pay attention to your elders.

Some people do just that. They figure anybody who has survived for so long in Alaska must know something worth knowing. So they listen carefully to any mumbling old duffer.

"What did he say?" one will ask.

"I think he said, 'Never run with scissors,'" another will reply.

"Gee, what wisdom," the first will say. "I'd better write that down."

Yeah, I know. There's not much hope for this younger generation. If they'll believe you, they'll believe anything. So the proper response is to have mercy on them. If they weren't young and foolish, they wouldn't be listening to you in the first place. So don't tell them that the path to true enlightenment can be reached only by carving a replica of the riverboat *Nenana* from a block of Velveeta. And for God's sake, don't give them your old hootchinoo recipe. They'll blow themselves to bits.

In most of Alaska, if you die in the winter, you can't be buried until spring. The ground's too frozen.

17 | Dying in the Far North

Or, If You Can't Go in Style, Why Make the Trip?

Despite the fresh air, vigorous activity, and sheer cussedness, even Alaskans die. They often die in peculiarly Alaska ways. They fall off mountains. Their snow machines break through the river ice. Nobody wants to go in their sleep, or drop dead from heart failure.

Everybody wants to die like a real Alaskan.

Except for the *real* Alaskans. They want to live forever.

Unfortunately, no one has managed that yet. And not everyone can count on a gloriously Alaska death. So, when you attend the funeral of another Alaskan, there are certain questions you should never ask the grieving family. Among them are: What was his blood-alcohol ratio? Is that his widow or his granddaughter? Who gets the old boy's dough? In fact, it's safer not to ask any questions at all.

Unless, of course, the deceased is someone you didn't like. Then, it's perfectly appropriate to say to the widow, "I suppose you're burying the old boy in his swim trunks."

"Why's that?" she'll ask.

"Well, I hear it's plenty hot where he's going," you'll say, "so the fewer clothes, the better."

A bit of witty repartee is acceptable, but no matter how much you disliked the deceased, do not laugh at the funeral. Don't even chortle. Not only is this bad form, everybody will ask you what's so funny. This will disrupt the funeral and delay the start of the wake.

A few other rules:

Do not show up drunk. When the minister asks if there are people in the audience who want to share their feeling about the deceased, you might get up and tell the truth. Big mistake. More important, showing up drunk implies you don't trust the grieving family to throw a proper wake. Because no Alaskan ever drinks his own booze if there's the faintest chance somebody else might be buying.

Do not hit on the widow. No matter how glad both of you are the old coot is dead, suggesting that you sneak off during the ceremony is bad form. Wait until the wake.

Make sure the deceased is dead. However, sticking the corpse with pins, giving it a hotfoot, and prying back its eyelids are frowned upon. Holding a mirror discreetly under its nostrils is acceptable, as is whispering that they've just struck gold on that worthless claim he no longer owns because he's dead. Of course, if he knocks you down scrambling out of his coffin at this news, you can't complain. Nobody would listen, anyway. They'd be too busy asking the former widow, "Does this mean the bar is closing?"

Certainly, you wouldn't want your own services to be a social disaster. Even if you can count on your doctor to make absolutely certain you are dead, and on your survivors to do the right thing, you should still make your own arrangements. If you die without leaving behind proper instructions, bad things can happen. Lawyers might get involved. There could be a church service. And they might serve soda pop at your wake.

Write a will that will offend everybody. Leave your worldly goods to the waitress at your favorite roadhouse. Send a sealed envelope to your best friend's wife, telling her what he did when the two of you were out of town at the last Pioneers' convention. And don't forget your relatives.

"And to my shiftless nephew, Elroy, who asked to be remembered in my will: I remember you, Elroy. You're a bum. Get a job."

Once you've fulfilled your social obligations, you have to outline the proper disposition of your body. In most of Alaska, if you die in the winter, you can't be buried until spring. The ground's too frozen. So, Like Sam McGee, many Alaskans ask for a warmer fate:

"Yet 'tain't being dead.
it's my awful dread of the icy grave
that pains;

So I want you to swear that,
foul or fair, you'll cremate
my last remains."

Or, you can choose to have your family stick you in the permafrost cellar until spring, provided you don't mind being folded a couple of times.

These aren't the important matters, anyway. What is important to understand is this:

The real purpose of an Alaskan will is to spell out the arrangements for the wake.

Oh, and the funeral, too.

Be precise about your pallbearers. If you want your casket carried by a dog team, six dance hall girls, or your worthless in-laws (because you want them to do a little work for a change), say so.

Specify the music you want. If you don't, they'll either play long-hair music you can't dance to, or those religious tunes you haven't heard since your mother hauled you to church by the ear. You don't want that. You will want music that is lively and upbeat. You should be asking yourself, *Rock the Casbah* when they bring the casket in, and *Funkytown* as they carry it out? Or the other way around?"

Spell out exactly what you want said. This is simple self-defense. If you don't write your own ceremony, they'll surely use the Biblical text about the prodigal son.

Be precise about who you want to perform the rites.
Much better to have your old prospecting partner do
the honors than some long-winded clergyman. You ever
met a man of the cloth who could tell the joke about the
miner, the moose, and the dance-hall girl right? Besides,
your partner will know what's important. He'll get everybody to the wake fast.

Here, of course, is the most important part of your
last will and testament: the plans for the wake. A mil-
lion questions must be answered. Hootchinoo or
store-bought liquor? Both? Live music or a DJ? Does
the chorus line sing *Bye, Bye Baby* before the fist fight or
after? An Alaskan can be remembered for many things.
But the wake is an Alaskan's last, and most important,
social obligation.

Well, second to last. There's your headstone. You
don't want to leave this job to just anybody. They'll put
your name, dates of birth and death, and some uplift-
ing inscription. Not the sort of thing an Alaskan wants
to be staring up at for eternity. How much better to leave
behind the kind of message that says there's an Alaskan buried here. People have their own ideas about how
to do that. Here's mine:

Dead, but still thirsty.

About the Author

Mike Doogan is a third-generation Alaskan born and raised in Fairbanks. He has spent his entire life in the 49th state, much of it just trying to stay warm. For the past thirty years, he has lived in Anchorage, making his living mainly as a journalist and writer. Among his writings are *Half-Baked Alaska*, a monthly humor column he wrote four years for *Alaska* magazine, *Dawson City*, published by the Alaska Geographic Society, and *How to Speak Alaskan*, published by Epicenter Press. He currently is an opinion columnist for the *Anchorage Daily News*, where he makes many of his fellow Alaskans hopping mad three times a week. His work has won a bunch of state and regional awards, as well as a share of the newspaper's 1989 Pulitzer Prize. He and his remarkably patient wife, Kathy, have been married 26 years and have two children, Matt and Amy. Although Doogan doesn't own a weasel or a wanigan, he has acquired an impressive jumble of camping gear.

More Humor from Epicenter Press